GOD'S
WORD
IN
TODAY'S
WORLD

GOD'S WORD IN TODAY'S WORLD

Suzanne de Dietrich

THE JUDSON PRESS, Valley Forge

GOD'S WORD IN TODAY'S WORLD
Copyright © 1967
The Judson Press, Valley Forge, Pa. 19481

Except where otherwise indicated, the Bible quotations in this volume are in accordance with the Revised Standard Version of the Bible, copyright 1946 and 1952, by the Division of Christian Education of the National Council of the Churches of Christ in the United States of America, and are used by permission.

Library of Congress Catalog Card No. 67-25894

Printed in the U.S.A.

PREFACE

"BIBLICAL IMPERATIVES FOR TODAY" was the assigned theme for the lectures out of which this little book has grown. But what does this mean? Biblical imperatives are always the same; God's promises and God's commandments do not change.

Nevertheless, in the Bible God speaks concretely to people of a given time. He speaks in their categories of thought, not in abstract generalities. We therefore need to reach the people of our own day by trying to speak their language and by stressing the needs and problems of the world in which we live.

Today, more than ever, we should be world conscious and try to face the problems of the people around us. We must be realistic and realize that more and more of them are detached from the Christian faith or have never heard of the Christian faith and that we are responsible to God for all those who are questioning our faith today. We must be aware of their problems and give some time to facing their questions and to searching for the answers.

SUZANNE DE DIETRICH

CONTENTS

The World's Challenge: "Where Is Thy God?"   11

God's Challenge: "Man, Where Are You?"   27

The Quest for Justice   43

The Quest for Freedom   61

The Quest for Truth   79

Christ, Our Hope   95

THE
WORLD'S
CHALLENGE:
"WHERE IS THY GOD?"

On a recent Easter morning, thousands of people gathered in front of the Moscow Cathedral and shouted: "God is dead!" But inside, other thousands greeted one another with the great Easter proclamation: "Christ is risen! He is risen indeed!"

That such things should happen in Soviet Russia is not surprising, but the slogan "God is dead" was not invented there. It was imported from the West. It was spoken by Nietzche nearly a century ago. Yet in our own day it has suddenly become the catchword not of professed atheists but of young people and even of some theologians who still claim to be Christian. Surely the movement is limited to a minority of young intellectuals, but its very existence is a sign of the times, and the secular press has given it wide publicity. It has spread throughout the United States and Western Europe. For instance, I quote from an article by Lee E. Dirks in the *National Observer:*

> The kettledrums shuddered, then rumbled ever louder in a powerful crescendo. "Why is there no dawn?" asked the reader in the requiem at North Carolina Wesleyan College. "Why do our dead only die? Why do our living only live?"

"Your God is dead!" cried the chorus as tears began to form in the eyes of the 600 students. "He died in the darkness of your image. . . . He died because you held his hand too tightly." Then, just before the final crash of the kettledrums, the chorus screamed the litany's stunning, apocalyptic words: *"God is dead!"*[1]

The author of the article goes on with the statement that "theological unrest is sweeping Protestantism" and that "paperbacks on theology are selling like Ian Fleming's espionage novels." That there is widespread uncertainty about the nature of God and the relevance of the biblical revelation is shown by the success of books like Bishop Robinson's *Honest to God* as well as by the stirring effect of the much more radical school of young theologians such as William Hamilton and Thomas J. J. Altizer. Altizer states his case clearly enough:

Surely it is not possible for any responsible person to think that we can any longer know or experience God in nature, in history, in the economic or political arenas, in the laboratory, or in anything which is genuinely modern, whether in thought or in experience. Wherever we turn in our experience, we experience the eclipse or the silence of God.[2]

At the same time, the tenants of this new theology insist on their allegiance to Jesus, the Word made flesh. But how can one believe in the Son while rejecting what constitutes the very basis of the Son's being, his faith in the Father?

My aim is not to discuss this theological trend, but we are bound to ask ourselves why it exerts such attraction on large groups among the young generation in most western countries. Just because we believe in the relevance of the biblical message for our time, we must try to understand where the stumbling block lies. Are we not partly responsible for the apparent misinterpretation of this message?

In a very fair analysis of this avant-garde theology, John

[1] *National Observer*, January 31, 1966.

[2] Quoted by John C. Bennett, "In Defense of God," *Look*, April 19, 1966, p. 70.

C. Bennett identifies three main motives "that cause sensitive and honest men to doubt the existence of God or to proclaim the absence of God," namely:

1. The growth of scientific knowledge: "God seems crowded out of the world most of us experience. . . ."

2. The problem of evil and suffering.

3. The need of some men to emancipate themselves from a God who seems to threaten their freedom and their dignity as responsible men (as in the case of Karl Marx) .[3]

Let us note, first of all, that none of these arguments is very new. The psalmist hears scoffers asking him continually, "Where is your God?" (Psalm 42). The question of evil and suffering is as old as the world. The Bible offers no ready-made solution for this problem; in fact, Job's friends are blamed by God himself for pretending to have their answers ready. The only answer the Bible offers is the cross, where God in Christ takes upon himself the burden of suffering and evil and death.

The longing of man to be the sole master of his destiny goes back as far as the old Genesis story of Adam and Eve, and as far as the Promethean dream of the Greeks who told of man's effort to steal fire from heaven. Still, however, we must ask ourselves why these questions have become so acute in our time.

It is certainly due, first of all, to the amazing development of science and technology in this century. Man has conquered the spaces. Biological research seems on the verge of discovering the secret of producing life. There seems to be no limit to the power of man to control the forces at work in this universe, to shape his own destiny. In fact, this power seems to have gone to his head! Where does God appear in such a picture?

One could object, of course, that the most serious scientists are much more aware of their human limits than

[3] Summarized from Bennett's article, *Ibid.*

the general public supposes. So many theories have been discarded because of new discoveries that a great scientist could say recently: "We know now that we know nothing." The great scientists have become very humble; it is the pseudo-scientists who are sure that they are going to know everything. One could also stress the fact that the scientists themselves are afraid of the consequences of their discoveries. They feel that man is not mature enough to handle his knowledge without the risk of ending in self-destruction.

There remains a certain mystery in this universe that no scientist pretends to solve, and there is less of a conflict between science and religion than a century ago, because science now acknowledges its limits and has become very empirical in its methods.

The real problem seems to me to lie at a deeper level. Daily life has become so absorbing, so full of new possibilities that God has been crowded out of our busy life, our work, our thought. The real question is whether our West is not gaining the world and losing its soul — whether we are not in process of losing that fourth dimension of life, the spiritual dimension, which gives all other dimensions their depth and meaning. The life of the Spirit implies silence, and people today are more and more afraid of silence. The life of the Spirit calls for the discipline of prayer and worship. The whole trend of our time runs counter to these things, however, and we all have to struggle against being carried away by the pace at which we live.

The first task of the church, assailed from without and within, is surely a deepening of her own thought and life. Whether we like it or not, we are part and parcel of this busy man-made, man-centered world; we share its doubts and problems. Moreover, we *should* share them. We *should* be involved.

The concern of the young generation which tries to express its faith in new ways has grown out of a determined will to understand and to serve the world-as-it-is, to face with an open mind the drastic changes which are taking place under our eyes. This is the positive side of their quest. Young people speak all the time of "going out into the world." They are concerned about the slums, about war, about civil rights — in fact, about all kinds of things which are going on in this world. They feel that the church is not conscious enough of such matters, and therefore they go away from the church into the world. They are often re- markably honest in their quest for truth, and they accuse us of not living up to what we profess. Should we not also recognize that their attack is directed against an all too widespread conception of God and religion which is too self centered?

There is a significant sentence in the student requiem I quoted a moment ago: God died "because you held his hand too tightly." Has not religion been conceived, all too often, as a haven of security in which people tried to escape from the problems of daily life? Religion can lull our fears, reassure our conscience, and provide an alibi for our sense of responsibility.

But such a religion has nothing to do with true Chris- tian faith. It provides the kind of security against which the prophets have spoken their most violent condemnation and which Jesus denounced as deadly. In such a conception God becomes *le Bon Dieu*, "the Good God," who takes over the responsibility for our lives, who is at our service rather than we at his. *He* is expected to fulfill *our* wishes. Is it not partly against this infantile concept of God that the young generation reacts? A child needs the security of the home, the care of the mother, the authority of the father. But a possessive mother, who goes on watching every step of the child and would (if she could) keep him a child forever, prevents his growth. Likewise a domi- neering father, whose ideal is to shape his son in his own image and likeness, either kills his son's personality and initiative or drives him to bitter revolt.

Have we not sometimes projected on God the image of the possessive mother or the domineering father? Is not the rebellion of the present young generation a psychological reaction against a certain concept of fatherhood?

"When I was a child," says Paul, "I spoke like a child, I thought like a child, I reasoned like a child; when I became a man, I gave up childish ways" (1 Corinthians 13:11). Such maturing is true also of faith. To say that man has come of age does not mean that he can dispense with God but that his relation to the Father will be that of a responsible adult. Who acts more responsibly than the prophet who dares to oppose all the authorities of his time in the name of the Holy God in whom he believes? The search for "religion" has been all too often a search for security, implying a certain social conformity to accepted customs and beliefs.

It has been rightly remarked, however, that the men of God are always *called out* of their secure haven and forced to tread unknown ways. Abraham leaves his clan, his traditions, his gods, to start the venture of faith: "He went out, not knowing where he was to go." Likewise, Moses leaves all the securities of a princely home in Egypt to start on his great solitary venture. Under his leadership the tribes are taken out of Egypt — out of captivity — but also away from the security of Egyptian fleshpots into the wilderness.

Faith is a venture in the unknown, the breaking away from earthly security, the total commitment of our life in the service of God and man. Faith is a responsible relationship: the reality of this relationship cannot be proved; it can only be lived.

It has been the temptation of medieval theology to appeal to reason in order to prove the existence of God, and subsequent theologies have not been completely free from such attempts. Such arguments meet today with growing skepticism, however. We can prove neither the existence of God nor his nonexistence by sheer logic, and the one effort is as futile as the other.

The Bible takes the existence of God for granted, but yet as a reality which must be grasped by faith. The Hebrew mind is remarkably free of speculations on the nature of God, those speculations so dear to Western philosophy. The God of the Bible can only be known insofar as he reveals himself through his Word, and this metaphor is the biblical way of saying that God speaks to the *heart of man*.

But every word of God is also *deed*. He is God-in-action. What he says, he does. He is a God who enters history, the history of a man, the history of a chosen people, through whom he unfolds his purpose for mankind.

The historical character of the biblical revelation is certainly one of the main difficulties of modern man in his approach to the biblical records. How can these old stories have any relevance for our twentieth-century problems in the era of highly developed techniques, the era of the cosmonauts and the atomic bomb? Some of these ancient stories are strange mixtures of history and saga. We must imagine the Israelites of old coming together around a fire in the evening and retelling the stories of their ancestors; and these stories become basic to their faith in the God who has led their ancestors. The encounters of God with man are told in the framework and are colored by the concepts of a primitive culture with which we have little in common. God speaks concretely, not in abstract or general terms. He was understood by these ancient people because he entered into their categories of thought, taking them where they were, as he mercifully takes us where we are.

The Bible is a more difficult book than some would be inclined to admit. The modern reader needs to be helped, and such help is the function of adult Bible study. Bible study on the adult level is important, because there are certain things you simply cannot tell a child, and the deeper theological meaning of the Bible should therefore be explained to adults. This is necessary if the adult is to discover the depth of meaning of these ancient stories and myths conveyed in a form which to the superficial reader, may seem anthropomorphic and naive. There is no deeper theologian, for instance, than the old Jahwist, who wrote chapters two and three of Genesis and so many of the stories, for he was tremendously aware of the living reality of the God who encounters man in real life, and he understood what constantly goes on in the heart of man.

We do not have to "demythologize" the Bible, but we are to interpret each story or event in the context in which it was written. The historical and exegetical work done in recent years has helped us greatly to see better in what time, in what precise situation each book of the Bible came to be written, and what message it was meant to convey to the people there and then. God's Word is not an abstract Word; it is directed to certain men faced with a definite situation. When we have grasped the message in the concrete realism of its own setting, we may well discover that there is a living Word for *us* and *our own day* in these old pages. The human heart remains the same, but a hasty and unwarranted transposition to our own circumstances may also be misleading. To pick out a verse and transplant it to our own situation where it does not correspond to the one in which it was spoken is wrong. This mistake has been made all too often.

Here another word of warning is needed. A Christian should read the Old Testament in the light of the New, that is, in the light of the fulfillment. Jesus claims that he came to fulfill, not to abolish the Law proclaimed by the fathers. But on certain points he opposes what was said "to the men of old" in the name of a higher revelation: "But I say to you" (Matthew 5:21-22 ff). When his disciples, inspired by the example of Elijah, suggest that he send down the fire of heaven on the Samaritans who refuse to receive him, Jesus rebukes them. Some manuscripts quote him saying: "You do not know what manner of spirit you are of" (Luke 9:55, note *f*). The old war-god of ancient Israel is no more the God of Jesus Christ. Unfortunately, however, in the history of the church, men have been all too glad to return to the Old Testament stories, and the old war-god has often come alive again, used to justify all the cruelties of war.

There is some truth in the ironical word of Voltaire: "God has made man in his own image, but man has paid him back!" We have described him at different times in history as a God of wrath who seems to enjoy sending people to hell, or again as a sentimental father too good to resent our failures. But such extremes betray the God of Jesus Christ, and he only can be the object of our faith and commitment.

The whole Bible is a story of *relationships*. Naturally, in the infancy stage, Israel would consider these in lesser terms than those of the mature prophets or our Lord himself. To those who consider the Bible as an antiquated book, however, I would say that my studies have led me to think that its approach is remarkably modern, just because it is a dynamic and realistic approach. It is a story from beginning to end of broken and restored relationships — between man and God and between man and man. We are forced with a choice, with a decision to be made here and now.

The relationship God builds is one of *faith*. Is this not true of any relationship? We can only discover who the other is by opening to him, by trusting him, by listening to him. If we do not listen, we cannot know him, for we will not go through to the depths of his soul. There must be a certain give-and-take in which our whole being (will, heart, and mind) is involved. To "know" someone, in biblical language, implies such an involvement of the total man. It means the insight of love. To know God implies trust, commitment, obedience. This is what the Bible means by faith.

The initiative of the relationship lies always with God, and it takes the form of a covenant. The very concept of covenant is one of the original features of the Hebrew and Christian faith. It stresses the responsible character of the relationship on both sides. The contract is offered by God and accepted by man.

The character of God is revealed in his faithfulness to the contract he has concluded with his people. He can never forsake his promises, as Paul says, "For the gifts and the call of God are irrevocable" (Romans 11:29). Man, on the other hand, is a free and responsible creature: He can reject God's offer or thwart God's purpose. Here lies the mystery of the God in whom we believe: that, while being totally free himself, yet he consents to limit his own freedom in order to call forth man's free response.

Faith is the act by which a man stakes his whole life on God's Word, whether this Word comes in the form of a promise, a call, or a commandment.

Why is Abraham so often mentioned in the New Testament, and first of all by Jesus himself? This old Bedouin, about whom we know so little, has become the prototype (should we say the archetype?) of faith. In a sense he incarnates the faith of Israel. "Abraham believed the Lord; and he reckoned it to him as righteousness" (Genesis 15:6, Romans 4:3). Is it not striking that Abraham should have become the claimed ancestor of the three religions that profess faith in a personal and living God — Judaism, Christianity, and Islam?

Faith, according to the eleventh chapter of the Letter to the Hebrews, is "the assurance of things hoped for, the conviction of things not seen." This chapter describes a kind of pilgrims' march toward the city to come, a procession of men walking in the path of history. The writer says, "These all died in faith, not having received what was promised, but having seen it and greeted it from afar." This is the great "cloud of witnesses" to whom God has become tremendously real as a power that entered their lives and changed their lives, gave them purpose and goal. The procession runs from Abel to Jesus Christ, who is described as "the pioneer and perfecter of our faith." With him a new procession begins: the procession of martyrs, prophets, and saints who keep the church alive as a church militant to this day. We should think of ourselves as surrounded by this host of witnesses and running our course in the arena under their eyes.

Were all these men, those who prepared the way for Christ's coming and those who followed him, victims of an illusion? Of course it is always possible to say so. The way remains for us as it was for them the way of faith, not of sight. To find out whether they are right or wrong we have to stake our all on God's promises. But these promises are now embodied in a human life: The Word has become flesh.

Jesus is the very exponent of absolute faith in God. His relation to the one he calls his Father is a relation of total trust and commitment. His oneness in will and purpose with the Father is the basic reality of his life and mission, but this submission is shown in the Gospels to be the free decision of a mature mind. In the story of the temptation Jesus is faced with the expectations of his people. He consciously rejects the possibility of becoming the political messiah that the crowds want him to be. He rejects the signs which might have convinced the Pharisees. He rejects all outward power. He deliberately chooses the way of the Suffering Servant and faces the consequences. His is a free choice. He lays down his life of his own accord (John 10:17-18).

His is the way of responsible sonship. He makes the redeeming purpose of God his own. He comes into this world to call us to the sonship of the children of God. But men remain free to respond to the call, to turn to the light or to turn away from the light (John 3:16-21). In faith, Jesus sees the day when all men will be drawn to him, and through him to the Father (John 12:32). But he also sees the possibility of rejection: "When the Son of man comes, will he find faith on earth?" (Luke 18:8).

Because God wants to build a world of responsible beings, and because he wants not puppets but sons who will respond freely to his love, the question remains open. God can do anything except force men to love him, for then it would be love no more.

To those who ask, "Where is your God?" Christians can only answer: He is the Holy God of righteousness and mercy who meets us in Jesus Christ. He is the God who became man to meet men in the concrete and bitter reality of their lives, so that in and through him they might grow to mature and true manhood.

We know him because "The Word of God is living and active, sharper than any two-edged sword, piercing to the division of soul and spirit, of joints and marrow, and discerning the thoughts and intentions of the heart. And before him no creature is hidden . . ." (Hebrews 4:12-13). To meet God is to be looked through.

We know him as one who strips off all our self-complacencies, all our illusions, and forces us to face the reality of our inmost being and of the world in which we live.

We know him as the Healer of our most secret wounds, as the one who calls us to newness of life, and in whom our lives have found a purpose and goal.

We know him as the Lord of history in whom the whole of creation tends toward its ultimate fulfillment. He who so loved the world that he gave his only Son for our salvation is not the God of the few who profess to believe in him: He will not rest until the whole of creation will meet its deliverance.

This is the God in whom we believe. He is not "up there" in the skies nor "out there" in some distant galaxy. No cosmonaut is going to find God in space unless he finds God in his heart—and if he finds him there he can do it as well back home on earth. We have learned nineteen centuries ago that "God is Spirit, and those who worship him must worship him in Spirit and truth" (John 4:24).

His Spirit dwells in the heart of the believer and its fruits are joy, peace, and the courage to live responsibly as a man among men.

GOD'S
   CHALLENGE:
"MAN, WHERE ARE YOU?"

WE GO TO THE BIBLE with many questions. But soon it is the Bible which questions us, and the fundamental question is *"Where are you?"* In other terms: What are you doing with your life? What are you heading for? Where do you stand in relation to God and your fellowmen?

The question "Where are you?" appears for the first time in the third chapter of Genesis. Adam and Eve have eaten the forbidden fruit of the tree of knowledge and they are hiding now from one another, from God, and from their own selves. They have snatched at equality with God and aimed at building a man-centered universe. They stand in a world of broken relationships; they have fallen into the loneliness of the ego.

One could well describe in this marvelous story the sudden situation of Adam and Eve as one of solitude. They were called to be one, and now they feel the need to hide. First they hide their bodies; then they run away from God into the bushes; and finally they accuse not themselves but each other for what has happened. It is a break of relationships. And God is shown looking around and asking, Where are you?" They were hiding.

The story is profound. We do stand in a world of broken relationships, a world where love has lost its transparency. There are blessed moments when we feel at one with another person we love — looking through that person's thoughts — but these are short. Most of the time we go on suffering from the fact that we never quite "get through." We are never quite known, and we never quite know the other person. He does not quite understand what we try to convey. We are, in a deep sense, alone. Man has become a stranger to man because we all wear masks; we all try to hide from the realities of life.

To be saved, we have to be unmasked. We have to face ourselves as we are and the world as it is. This is why the same question "Where are you?" runs all through the Bible. Adam and Eve, where are you? Cain, where are you? Builders of the Babel towers of the world, where are you? Kings and empires who once possessed the world, where are you? Israel, where are you? Judah, where are you? Church of God, where are you today in this troublesome world? Men and women of the twentieth century, proud inventors of the atomic bomb, proud dominators of the world, where are you?

The question rings in our ears. What is man, O God, in thy sight? Toward what destiny is he heading? As we consider this crucial question, let us turn to the biblical view of man.

The Bible is realistic in its view of man. Man is seen as part of nature, still close to the animal world and yet at the same time unique because of his relation to God. In both of the creation stories, creation is seen as the setting of the stage where the history of man with God will unfold itself. Israel was first conscious of the living God who was acting in her own history, and at a later stage she became aware that this was the God of *all* history. It is this history that gives meaning to creation.

Science tells us today that the formation of our planet took billions of years and that the first man appeared probably 500,000 years ago. Of course, the biblical writers were ignorant of modern geology and archeology. But the seven days of Genesis 1 are symbolic of a long and complete process, the culmination of which was to be the creation of man. The number seven in the ancient world is a symbol of completeness.

The Jahwist account in Genesis 2 and 3 tells us that man was made of the dust of the ground and will return to dust. His physical life shares the fate of all creatures; short and precarious is its span. The brevity and fragility of human life is deeply felt by the psalmist:

> As for man, his days are like grass;
>   he flourishes like a flower of the field;
> for the wind passes over it, and it is gone,
>   and its place knows it no more.
> But the steadfast love of the Lord is from everlasting to everlasting
>   . . . (Psalm 103:15-17).

The Preacher in the book of Ecclesiastes echoes in a strange way the modern skeptic:

> I said in my heart with regard to the sons of men that God is testing them to show them that they are but beasts. For the fate of the sons of men and the fate of beasts is the same; as one dies, so dies the other. They all have the same breath, and man has no advantage over the beasts; for all is vanity. All go to one place; all are from the dust, and all turn to dust again. Who knows whether the spirit of man goes upward and the spirit of the beast goes down to the earth? (Ecclesiastes 3:18-21)

The compilers of the Bible were not afraid of including in its literature this piece of antique wisdom. We are reminded that man is not immortal by his nature, that he is still part of the animal world.

What, then, makes man unique in the whole of creation? The Jahwist answers: his relation to God, the fact that God "speaks" to his heart and entrusts to him his garden. It is this I—Thou relationship which lifts man above the animal level and makes him a responsible being.

The later, Priestly tradition goes a step further, saying that man and woman are created *in the image and likeness of God*. And they are given, in togetherness, *dominion over God's creation*.

Many explanations have been given of this Priestly text. Did the author see the whole created world as God's temple, and man at the center as God's representative, the guardian of the temple, his earthly statue of clay? Did the inspired writer have some foreboding of the deeper meaning of the *imago Dei* as the ultimate destiny of man? The New Testament sees in Christ the true *imago Dei*, into the likeness of which we are to be transformed. To this idea we shall return.

But first we should consider further the concept of stewardship implied in this passage. God is seen as entrusting creation to man for man's use and enjoyment. He gives man dominion over the whole created world (Genesis 1:26). When, in our own day, man explores the depths of the earth and of the seas, ventures into outer space, acquires more and more scientific knowledge and technical skill, all this can be considered as part of his calling. All this can be done to the glory of God and for the benefit of mankind.

The difficulty does not lie in science as such but in the discrepancy between man's power and man's spiritual maturity. I recall the story of Tubal-cain, who is said in Genesis 4:22 to have forged the first instruments of bronze and iron, a discovery of as decisive importance for primitive mankind as that of nuclear fission for the modern world. The immediate consequence is a triumph song of Lamech, who now can kill "seventy-sevenfold" more people than Cain did before him. Is not the story repeating itself in our own day with the atomic bomb? The sole difference is that our power of destruction has become limitless and

Lamech's looks now as child's play. Mankind does not change much.

How clearly our old Bible describes the possibilities for both good and evil that man possesses. Is he not, from beginning to end, the apprentice sorcerer who claims to hold the world in his hands and finally may well run to his own destruction? Is man really "come of age," as some say? Is not, rather, the vertigo of power the same, but enlarged to fearful dimensions? Is it not still the adamic temptation to dominate rather than to serve, to be the little self-centered god of our surroundings — a temptation which appears in ever-new forms but at bottom remains the same? Is not the tower of Babel the symbolic illustration of the adamic dream transferred to the collectivity? Is not political prestige with its display of power one of the devilish forces of our own time? Are we not more interested in ourselves than in anybody else?

The greatness of man lies in the fact that he is called to be God's co-worker in the process of creation. But he remains free to enter into God's design or to thwart it. And the whole Old Testament is a long story of revolts and returns, "for the imagination of man's heart is evil from his youth" (Genesis 8:21).

One last comment before we leave the Genesis stories: Man is conceived from the beginning as man-in-community. The couple is the first nucleus of the larger community which is to be. The two are called to be one. And all the successive covenants that God will call into being will strive to build or to restore community. Already in the Old Testament the relation to God and to neighbor are two aspects of the same reality.

The revelation of God's relation to man finds a further expression in the Psalms. Psalm 8, for instance, is one of the most beautiful expressions of man's position before God, both so humble and so great:

When I look at the heavens, the work of thy fingers,
  the moon and the stars which thou hast established;
what is man that thou art mindful of him,
  and the son of man that thou dost care for him?

Yet thou hast made him little less than God,
  and dost crown him with glory and honor.
Thou hast given him dominion over the works of thy hands;
  thou hast put all things under his feet,
all sheep and oxen,
  and also the beasts of the field,
the birds of the air, and the fish of the sea,
  whatever passes along the paths of the sea.

O Lord, our Lord,
  How majestic is thy name in all the earth!

The greatest wonder of the believer is not to know God but to *be known* of him, as we read in Psalm 139:

O Lord, thou hast searched me and known me!
Thou knowest when I sit down and when I rise up;
  thou discernest my thoughts from afar. . . .

Whither shall I go from thy Spirit?
  Or whither shall I flee from thy presence?
If I ascend to heaven, thou art there! . . .
If I take the wings of the morning
  and dwell in the uttermost parts of the sea,
even there thy hand shall lead me,
  and thy right hand shall hold me.
If I say, "Let only darkness cover me,
  and the light about me be night,"
even the darkness is not dark to thee,
  the night is as bright as the day;
  for darkness is as light to thee.

For the psalmist, God is not someone "up there" or "out there"; he is a mysterious omnipresence who dwells in the heart of man — a presence that fills man with adoration and awe. How great is this God who gives him his body as well as his soul!

Here we have again a typical feature of the Hebrew understanding of man: Man is seen in his oneness as body, psyche (or soul), and spirit. All three are gifts of God. It is under Greek, not Hebrew, influence that Christianity has tended to look upon the flesh as the seat of evil. In the Bible the seat of evil lies in the heart, and the body is one of the great gifts of God's creation. Thus the Song of Solomon, the Canticle of Canticles, that beautiful song of human love, has been included in the canon of sacred literature! Of course, the church has spiritualized it and said it is an image of God's or Christ's relationship with his church, but it began as a real love song.

The ideal of the Hebrew is one of wholeness: wholeness of body and soul, health of the individual, and health of the community. When the Hebrew thinks of a new creation, he sees it as a place where people enjoy all the good things of life (Isaiah 65:17-25). Man is never thought of in isolation, but as part of a larger entity, the family, the clan, the tribe, the nation.

It is noteworthy that medical research today stresses more and more the fundamental interaction of body with physical and mental life and confirms at this point the biblical understanding of man as a whole. We are also more aware of the bearing of social disruption on the mental and physical health of the individual.

Israel underwent such disruption in the tenth and ninth centuries B.C. when it passed from the tribal stage to that of a nation. This involved a drastic change not only in the social and economic condition of the common people but in their religious life and human relationships. So deep was the crisis that for a while it seemed that the old faith would be lost, as old structures were breaking down and power and money became the main concern of the rulers. God called the prophets and made a new beginning, but the nation was reduced to a remnant.

We are faced today with more drastic changes than those of the time of David and Solomon. It is sometimes said that the technical revolution which is only beginning will go so far that the very nature of man will be changed. Are not some biologists claiming the possibility of modifying and "improving" his physical and mental capacities? Are not the prospective studies of some specialists foreseeing the total planning of the planet? But we need not look so far. One cannot visit Africa today without feeling the tremendous tensions between two worlds, two ways of living. Here too the tribal traditions are swiftly breaking down under the pressure of our Western techniques and the move from rural to urban life. People are torn between their allegiance to the clan and its customs and the new world opening before their all-too-wondering eyes. They still feel surrounded by the old forces of nature; they are afraid of these forces, of demons and taboos, of the wandering spirits of the dead. They crowd into the big cities of the coast, where they are lonely, lost, separated from the sociological setting in which they have grown up without having found a new basis on which to build their personal and common life. Will there be enough men of faith to carry these people through this present turmoil, as did the prophets of old?

And what about our Western world? In our plural society the old communities, the village, the parish, are breaking down, and an increasing number of men and women feel lost. Every man and woman lives several lives — in the home, in the profession, in the city, and in the church, for instance — often unconnected with each other.

It is a real possibility that many of the breakdowns we witness today are due to the tensions of human beings torn by several allegiances, several kinds of life, several codes of behavior, and sometimes not knowing where they stand as they struggle under these tensions. Only the discipline of a strong faith can maintain our basic unity, as revealed to us in Christ in this world of swift change and strife.

The pre-exilic Israel was carried away by the trends of the time, by its pagan surroundings. Post-exilic Israel, on the other hand, went to the other extreme. It succumbed to the clan-spirit, closing its eyes to the wider world. This withdrawal, alas, also may happen to us as we seek our self-preservation by becoming a closely-knit group which is afraid of the world. But this is a betrayal of our vocation. For we have been set apart, not for our own sakes but as God's holy priesthood standing before him for the nations, and standing as his witness among the nations. Once Israel stood as a unit, but at a still later stage, when the dispersion came, new forms of witness had to be found. Thus the church, called by Peter "a new race, a holy priesthood," was made of tiny groups scattered in a hostile world but made one through the new life in the Holy Spirit and boldly witnessing to their faith.

Let us summarize briefly our findings. The Old Testament leaves us with a vision of man as great because of his calling as God's steward on earth, created in God's image and yet soon lost when left to his own devices. It is man called to fullness of life but thwarting again and again God's saving purpose. This is a realistic picture which allows no illusion, but also is charged with hope. The faithfulness of God is experienced again and again, as a stiff-necked people are repeatedly brought back from their wanderings. And this man is man-in-community, learning painfully the conditions to be met if life in togetherness is to be made possible.

The New Testament shares the view of the Old concerning the destiny of man. It stresses even more strongly his lostness. The good news is that Jesus came to save the *lost;* contrary to the story of the prodigal son, Jesus leaves the house of the Father to find the younger brother and bring him back, at the cost of his own life.

No one has analyzed the condition of man more sharply than Paul:

> I do not understand my own actions. For I do not do what I want, but I do the very thing I hate. . . . So I find it to be a law that when I want to do right, evil lies close at hand. For I delight in the law of God, in my inmost self, but I see in my members another law at war with the law of my mind and making me captive to the law of sin which dwells in my members. Wretched man that I am! Who will deliver me from this body of death? Thanks be to God through Jesus Christ our Lord! (Romans 7:15, 21-25).

It is this split personality of man that Jesus restores to wholeness. When he asks the demoniac his name, the demoniac says, "We are legion," for man is several people at the same time. The healing of the body is only the first step in the process. The main step is the forgiveness of sin. It is the *total* man who is to be restored to his dignity as the child of God.

Jesus has been described as "the man for other men." He appears on the scene of history as one totally dedicated to God and man. He is open to all suffering and mainly to those for whom the hardships of life have thrown off the fellowship of their fellowmen, such as the outcast, the publican, the Samaritan, the prostitute. Only the self-righteous find him merciless. He deals with people as persons; he restores in them a sense of dignity and responsibility. He acts as neighbor to all those whom he meets.

In Jesus we have the revelation of mature manhood, of the image of God that man was called to be. In him our true destiny is revealed and is meant to be fulfilled.

We are thus presented with two images of man: the adamic and the Christlike. Adam is the prototype of the self-centered man, essentially (in spite of many masks) concerned with his own benefit and success. His god is

Adam — Adam's satisfaction, Adam's prestige, Adam's advancement in his profession and other spheres of life, Adam's power over others. Jesus is "the man for others," selfless and free, whose aim in life is not to dominate but to serve. Adam, with all his lusts, is still alive in every one of us. The very goal of Christian life is the passing from the one image to the other. This is the mysterious work of the Holy Spirit.

The change begins on earth, and it will attain its fulfillment at the end of time. Here again let us quote the apostle Paul:

> The first man was from the earth, a man of dust; the second man is from heaven. As was the man of dust, so are those who are of the dust; and as is the man of heaven, so are those who are of heaven. Just as we have borne the image of the man of dust, we shall also bear the image of the man of heaven (1 Corinthians 15:47-49).

How does this new life begin? Paul links it with baptism, which is here understood as symbolizing a real profession of faith.

> We were buried . . . with him [Christ] by baptism into [his] death, so that as Christ was raised from the dead by the glory of the Father, we too might walk in newness of life (Romans 6:4).

By the mysterious identification of redemptive love, Christ takes upon himself all we are, in order to make us all he is. He nails on the cross our old adamic self, so that it may die and we may be born again to a new life in the strength of his victory over sin and death.

The aim and goal of human life is to be conformed to the image of the Son (Romans 8:29). This purpose is the foundation of all of Christian ethics and should in fact be the foundation of our whole Christian thought and life.

The apostolic vision takes cosmic dimensions. Jesus is seen not only as the Savior of individual men but as the one in whom the whole created world finds its ultimate significance:

He is the image of the invisible God, the first-born of all creation; for in him all things were created, in heaven and on earth, visible and invisible, whether thrones or dominions or principalities or authorities — all things were created through him and for him. He is before all things, and in him all things hold together (Colossians 1:15-17).

This is a great and difficult passage. The whole meaning of the long history of our world, according to this passage, is to build up a mankind which will be the image of Christ, a "new creation" growing into his likeness (see also 2 Corinthians 5:14-15, 17-21; Ephesians 4).

Are these great affirmations of the apostolic faith less believable in the twentieth century than they were in the first? Whether there are many galaxies or one, the ultimate mystery of the world remains. The crux of the biblical revelation is that at the heart of the universe there is a redeeming love, leading the history of mankind to an ultimate fulfillment. It tells us that man is made for God, called to a mature manhood of which the measure is given to us in Christ. We are still "man in the making," still subhuman, slowly advancing toward that fullness of life of which, in our moments of faith, we have the premonition and the foretaste.

The Bible never claims that this vision of man's destiny in Christ is self-evident. It is a vision of faith. The Holy Spirit seals this faith in our hearts. It is a reality to be lived, and as we live it the day comes when we can say, "I know in whom I have believed," because we have experienced the reality and faithfulness of God in our own life.

What does this vision of man and of God's kingdom mean in relation to our attitude to the concrete problems of our own time? We live a period of swift change, of tremendous scientific development. For a Christian the first and crucial question will always be: What does all this do to *man* as a man? How does it improve or weaken his sense of responsibility, his human dignity? Does it strengthen or endanger his deeper life? Is the present trend of society in keeping with our Lord's concern for every child of God, with his lordship over all life? We shall discuss at a later stage some broader aspects of this problem. At this point, however, we shall limit ourselves to the personal aspect, and mention a few specific issues.

No one will deny the need for social welfare. But, as our world becomes more and more organized, such values as personal relationships and direct responsibility for one's relative or neighbor tend to be minimized. Man tends to become a cog in both the economic and the social machine. The stronger the organization, the less personal will be the relationship. Ten people care for the same patient in a modern hospital, but to each of them he is only "number such and such." The old relationship between nurse and patient is broken. This is only a tiny example of the trend we are facing today in all realms of life. The Christian's inventiveness and love will be needed if we are to maintain genuine brotherliness and the human touch in our welfare work, in our big housing projects, and throughout a highly organized and cold world.

It is true that our standards of living have improved, and this trend is a blessing. But do we not see every day that material wealth is not yet happiness? Other dimensions of life are needed. Why is it that the country of Europe where these standards are highest (Sweden) is also the one where the rate of suicide is one of the highest? Why, for so many young people today, is life not worth living? Shall we be able to stir all the possibilities which lie in them for constructive service to man?

Let us now revert to the question with which we started: Where are we? On what image of man have we staked our own lives? What are the goals toward which we strive?

What do we really long for, pray for? Are our own hearts not still divided between earthly success and the will to serve? Where do we stand as responsible beings answerable to God for his creation at this turning point of history? Where do we stand as his church? as responsible citizens of our nation and of the world at large? as members of a local community? These are some of the questions we should raise when we hear God say to us: "Where art thou?" "Where is thy brother?"

It is for every one of us to answer for himself.

THE
    QUEST
  FOR
JUSTICE

THE QUEST FOR JUSTICE AND FREEDOM has deeply marked modern history. It is the driving factor in the French and the American revolutions. Since the English industrial revolution of the last century, social and economic justice has been the standing claim of the world of labor. It has inspired Karl Marx's manifesto and the whole communist movement. Today, social and economic justice is the outcry of the countries which have suffered from exploitation by the richer countries of the world, the outcry of Asia, of Africa, of South America. This problem is the most burning one of our time and the most difficult to solve.

Has the Bible any message for us in this realm?

It is impossible to study the Bible without being struck by the considerable usage of legal terminology all through it. The word "justice" (or "righteousness") and other words derived from the same root appear no less than five hundred times in the Book. We have already stressed the fact that this vocabulary is meant to underline the responsible position of man before God. The covenant is conceived as a contract established by God with his people which embraces not only human relationships but man's use of

45

earthly goods as well. Any breach of contract calls forth the judgment of God.

In our Western world, the word "justice" sounds legalistic. Under the influence of Roman law we interpret it in terms of sheer equity: "To every one what belongs to him." The biblical concept of righteousness, however, goes far deeper; it has a religious connotation. It means basically a straight relationship between God and man, man and man. God's righteousness is manifested in his faithfulness to the covenant, in his victories over Israel's enemies. In the book of Judges, for instance, the victories of Israel are sometimes identified by the term "God's righteousness." This faithfulness is further manifested in God's judgments over his own people when they drift astray. Such judgment is not an end in itself but a drastic means to restore the right relationship, to build up a nucleus of the faithful who will carry on their God-given mission among the nations. It is a cutting-off of the withered branches so that the tree may go on bearing fruit.

Life under God implies straightforwardness and equity in human relationships. In the mosaic law, God appears again and again as the defender of the defenseless (the widow, the orphan, the stranger), as the protector of the poor. To this day this concept has helped the Jews to keep a strong sense of solidarity.

Wherever the tribal system exists, the tribe is a knit unit in which the needy are cared for. I am impressed with the way in which, for instance, African workers in Paris cling to one another, especially those of the same tribe or village. They share with one another, as those who have jobs carry those who are out of work. I have been told of one such group living in a cellar, because lodgings are a great problem, who have elected a chief and place all their money in a common fund. One-third goes to the families at home, one-third is for emergencies, and one-third is for the immediate needs of the group such as lodging and food. Similar practices were probably followed in the tribal life of Israel. Israel is no exception in this realm, but to her this care is uniquely a commandment of God. Duty toward God and duty toward neighbor can never be separated.

The hymns of enthronement of the kings show justice as the main attribute of the ruler:

> Give the king thy justice, O God,
>   and thy righteousness to the royal son!
> May he judge thy people with righteousness,
>   and thy poor with justice!
> Let the mountains bear prosperity for the people,
>   and the hills, in righteousness!
> May he defend the cause of the poor of the people,
>   give deliverance to the needy,
>   and crush the oppressor! . . .
>
> In his days may righteousness flourish,
>   and peace abound, till the moon be no more! (Psalm 72:1-4, 7)

When Israel becomes a nation, some drastic changes take place in the social and political structures. The old traditions tend to disappear. Israel seeks her security no more in the faithfulness of Yahweh but in the strength of her army and in the riches of her commerce. It is at this crucial moment of rapid social change that a new voice is heard: the voice of Israel's great prophets.

The appearance in Israel of the great prophets of the eighth and seventh centuries B.C. is a unique phenomenon in world history. Here are men who in the name of Holy God dare to challenge king, priest, and false prophet, and to proclaim doom to a flourishing nation. Israel is accused of having prostituted herself to foreign gods; she has forsaken the covenant. There is no justice in the land. The call is first a call to repentance, but a moment comes when the prophet knows that a new beginning is needed, that there is no return. Judgment is ahead and can no more be avoided. Only a remnant will be saved. But God never leaves his people without a future and a hope, and thus the messianic expectation dawns on the horizon.

It is not my purpose to analyze all aspects of the prophetic message but rather to show the prophets' burning concern for social and international justice. The first attacks of Amos are directed against the foreign nations which have transgressed the rules of warfare, as commonly accepted at that time:

> Thus says the Lord:
> "For three transgressions of Damascus,
>   and for four, I will not revoke the punishment;
> because they have threshed Gilead
>   with threshing sledges of iron . . ." (Amos 1:3).

The enumeration goes on for a whole chapter. Here Amos speaks of foreign nations who do not know Yahweh, but who also have a certain code of behavior. Certain things in war should not be done, for instance, because they are *cruel.* Even in those times that we are inclined to think of as primitive and backward, there were limits set to the ruthlessness of warfare.

The significance of this chapter lies in the fact that God is newly seen not only as the Lord of Israel's history but as one before whom all nations are answerable for their deeds, and woe on those who have cast off all pity! As Amos has been chanting his prophecies in the streets, the people have been quite happy to hear him sing doom on foreign nations. But suddenly he turns around, and God's wrath is directed to his own people. Because they know more, their responsibility is deeper. Nations who claim to have Christian rulers and Christian codes of behavior should always bear in mind these words of Amos:

> Thus says the Lord:
>   "For three transgressions of Israel,

and for four, I will not revoke the punishment;
because they sell the righteous for silver,
    and the needy for a pair of shoes —
they trample the head of the poor into the dust of the earth,
    and turn aside the way of the afflicted . . ." (Amos 2:6-7).

Here the judgment is on a deeper level. The main sin lies
in the social realm. But it is at the same time a sin of
ingratitude towards God, whose mercies are forgotten:

"You only have I known
    of all the families of the earth;
therefore I will punish you
    for all your iniquities . . ." (Amos 3:2).

Because you are near to my heart, he is saying, because I
have called you, because I have chosen you, you stand
under a more severe judgment, though the judgment is
part of my holy love.

Seek good, and not evil,
    that you may live;
and so the Lord, the God of hosts, will be with you,
    as you have said.
Hate evil, and love good,
    and establish justice in the gate . . . (Amos 5:14-15).

Amos is ruthless in his condemnation of a piety that is
not translated in terms of daily life and social justice:

"I hate, I despise your feasts,
    and I take no delight in your solemn assemblies. . . .
Take away from me the noise of your songs;
    to the melody of your harps I will not listen.
But let justice roll down like waters,
    and righteousness like an everflowing stream" (Amos 5:21, 23-24).

The prophet has stood in the market place and witnessed
the greed and dishonesty of the merchants. He has listened
to the judgments rendered by the judges at the gate. He
looks at the traffic of the world with open eyes. He is a
layman, a shrewd layman who knows what he is talking
about. The outward prosperity of Jeroboam's kingdom

cannot fool him. He sings a song of doom for Israel — a
funeral song. He knows that at bottom something is rotten
in the life of this nation. A people who forsake righteousness cannot live long. Amos foresees a time when there will
be a famine in the land, not of bread but "of hearing the
words of the Lord."

"They shall wander from sea to sea,
  and from north to east;
they shall run to and fro, to seek the word of the Lord,
  but they shall not find it.

"In that day the fair virgins and the young men
  shall faint for thirst . . ." (Amos 8:12-13).

These simple words of Amos remind us of the world today,
both East and West, full of young people who run to and
fro seeking an answer to the riddle of life and do not find it.
The worst judgment that the prophet forecasts is this
silence of God.

Micah, the man from the land, reacts against the city
man in frustration over the hard living of rural people
which is of benefit mainly to those in the cities. He thun-
ders against the rulers

who abhor justice
  and pervert all equity,
who build Zion with blood
  and Jerusalem with wrong (Micah 3:9-10).

Isaiah, a nobleman close to the court of the King, sees
the daughter of Zion "left like a booth in a vineyard"
(Isaiah 1:8). He cries:

Woe to those who join house to house,
  who add field to field,
until there is no more room,
  and you are made to dwell alone
  in the midst of the land.
The Lord of hosts has sworn in my hearing:
"Surely many houses shall be desolate,
  large and beautiful houses, without inhabitant . . ." (Isaiah 5:8-9).

We cannot easily read Isaiah's words without thinking of the big proprietors in Hungary after World War II; of some parts of Spain today where many people dwell on the land in misery and hunger while powerful individuals who own that land live in affluence; of Brazil, where there is tremendous resistance against the landowners who often spend their time and money somewhere on the Cote d'Azure while the poor peon is half starved on the land. It is no wonder that many people in Brazil are seeking a social revolution.

But the prophets have more to say to us. After the exile, when the country is in process of reconstruction and the people tend to become an ingrown, pious, self-centered community, another voice denounces all this fasting and lip service.

> "Is not this the fast that I choose:
>> to loose the bonds of wickedness,
>> to undo the thongs of the yoke,
> to let the oppressed go free,
>> and to break every yoke?
> Is it not to share your bread with the hungry,
>> and bring the homeless poor into your house;
> when you see the naked, to cover him,
>> and not to hide yourself from your own flesh?
> Then shall your light break forth like the dawn,
>> and your healing shall spring up speedily;
> your righteousness shall go before you,
>> the glory of the Lord shall be your rear guard.
> Then you shall call, and the Lord will answer;
>> you shall cry, and he will say, Here I am . . ." (Isaiah 58:6-9).

When all was well, Amos proclaimed doom; but now that judgment has happened, when Jerusalem has been taken and the people are in exile, a new note is being struck, the great note of hope. Our problem sometimes is that the church speaks *post eventum,* proclaiming doom when things are bad and hope when they are good, but the prophets did the reverse. Thus the hope of the prophets is turned towards the future, towards the coming of the Messiah. The characteristics of his reign will be justice and peace.

"Behold my servant, whom I uphold,
  my chosen, in whom my soul delights;
I have put my Spirit upon him,
  he will bring forth justice to the nations.
He will not cry or lift up his voice,
  or make it heard in the street;
a bruised reed he will not break,
  and a dimly burning wick he will not quench;
  he will faithfully bring forth justice.
He will not fail or be discouraged
  till he has established justice in the earth;
  and the coastlands wait for his law" (Isaiah 42:1-4).

This hunger and thirst for justice takes the most concrete forms. The new creation that the prophet expects will be one where all will enjoy the fruit of their labor:

"They shall build houses and inhabit them;
  they shall plant vineyards and eat their fruit.
They shall not build and another inhabit;
  they shall not plant and another eat . . ." (Isaiah 65:21-22).

These are very concrete expectations. They are echoed in some of the Negro spirituals. How the long-suffering of an exploited people rings through these words! How deeply engraved in their souls is the messianic hope!

"For I the Lord love justice,
  I hate robbery and wrong . . ." (Isaiah 61:8).

We have seen that the unfaithfulness of the leaders and people of Israel is the first target of prophetic utterances. But the world of nations also stands under judgment. The wrath of God is directed upon the conquerors who exert merciless oppression on the conquered people. Their main sin is pride; they act as if they were God himself and held the destiny of all nations in their hands. With bitter irony the prophets announce their downfall. How fragile are great empires which once dominated the world — Assyria, Babylonia, Persia, all rising and then falling!

Ezekiel presents us with a marvelous description of the wealth and beauty of Tyre, the queen of the seas. And yet she is doomed. Her king has thought of himself as a god, but he will be thrust down into the pit! The beautiful city will be turned to ashes:

> "You were blameless in your ways
>> from the day you were created,
>> till iniquity was found in you.
> In the abundance of your trade
>> you were filled with violence, and you sinned . . ."
>
> (Ezekiel 28:15-16).

In beautiful pages which one would like to quote in full, the prophet sees the king of Babylonia going down to dwell among the dead in Sheol, welcomed with amazement by his predecessors:

> " 'Is this the man who made the earth tremble,
>> who shook kingdoms,
> who made the world like a desert
>> and overthrew its cities,
>> who did not let his prisoners go home?' . . ." (Isaiah 14:16-17).

How actual all this sounds! Have we not seen in our own lifetime an empire which claimed to last for a millenium rise and fall in a decade? Does not our contemporary history show the fragility of all man-made empires?

The insights of the prophets into the history of their own time were not dictated first of all by outward events but by their vision of God as Lord of history. God is not mocked. They know that, sooner or later, unrighteousness bears its bitter fruits of strife and death. They know how the vertigo of power can carry a nation to the point of self-destruction.

We have said at the beginning that the message of the prophets was first a message of doom, yet one which pointed to a new beginning, to a new dawn. Here the mysterious figure of the Suffering Servant, as found in Isaiah, comes into the picture. He will establish justice on earth. But there is a new note: He will do so through the vicarious suffering of the just for the unjust (Isaiah 52, 53). This idea seems at first sight in contradiction with our whole concept of justice, our very human conception of "each his due." But the Hebrew people learned all through their history that God's ways are different; it is the presence and self-offering of the faithful few which save the unfaithful from utter annihilation.

Moses fights a lonely fight to deliver his people, and it is his faith that breaks open the way to freedom for all. He carries the sins of his people as his own and refuses to be saved without them. Thus when the people make a golden calf to worship, Moses asks God that he may share their punishment (Exodus 32:30-32). And when they are unfaithful and murmuring against God because they have no water, Moses strikes the rock and gives them water. Yet, because of *their* unfaithfulness and doubt at that time, God later does not allow *him* to enter the promised land; he who has been faithful bears the sin of those who have not. Jeremiah too bears heavily in his heart the sins of his nation, and because he opposes the policy of king and leaders, he is thrown into a pit; but his faith paves the way for a future restoration. In other terms, such is the deep solidarity of the people of God that the part represents the whole, and the man of God suffers vicariously for the nation.

It is with all this in mind that we should read Isaiah 53. Whether the prophet who wrote this great chapter had a prophet's tragic fate before his eyes, whether he thought of Israel as God's elect, suffering among the foreign nations and for their sake, remains an open question. These two interpretations are held by most Jews to this day. But for Christians the messianic interpretation of this text imposes itself. There is only one Righteous who really can take upon himself the plight of the unrighteous, our Lord Jesus Christ. In him the mysterious destiny of the so-called righteous of the Old Testament finds its ultimate fulfillment. He makes himself one with us so that through his victory we can become one with him and recover our true relation with Holy God.

Here the word "righteousness," understood as a straight relationship between sinful man and Holy God, takes its full depth of meaning: Righteousness can only be restored in this sinful world of ours by vicarious love.

The true relationship between God and man is one of trust and love. Through his obedience unto death, Jesus opens before us the possibility of a new life, the joyful life of the children of God. The apostle Paul calls Christ "our righteousness," and rightly so, because in him and through him we are reconciled to God, restored to our true relation to him. We stand before the mystery of the Cross. Yet, while never forgetting the uniqueness of our Lord's sacrifice for mankind, we should retain the message of solidarity that the Old Testament expresses so strongly. Christ's battle against the forces of evil goes on in this world to the end of time, and he has warned his disciples that they would have to share in his sufferings. Paul is aware that he is called to suffer for the sake of the churches, and he dares to say: "In my flesh I complete what is lacking in Christ's afflictions for the sake of his body, that is, the church" (Colossians 1:24). It is for the few who love God to offer themselves continually for those who do not know him.

"God was in Christ reconciling the world to himself, not counting their trespasses against them, and entrusting to us the message of reconciliation" (2 Corinthians 5:19). The prophets knew that the new creation, the reign of justice and love, could come only through an act of God. For us

Christians the secret of all reconciliation between God and man and between man and man lies in Christ's self-offering. This reconciliation we are to proclaim and live.

But here a difficult question comes up: What is the relation between this mystery of the faith, our reconciliation in Christ, and all we have seen about the prophetic message of justice? about their concept of history? Is this concept missing from the New Testament?

The Bible always pictures our relation to God and our relation to our fellowmen as two aspects of the same God-given reality. When our Lord said, "Blessed are those who hunger and thirst for righteousness, for they shall be satisfied" (Matthew 5:6), he surely thought of both our relation to God and to our fellowmen. Some try to limit righteousness to one of these relationships, some to the other, but such limitations are too narrow. Jesus was severe toward the rich who do not care for the poorer brother and definitely showed prophetic concern for social justice. He blamed his disciples for not discerning the signs of the times. A Christian will have no illusions as to the relativity of all human efforts toward more justice on earth. He does not expect to bring about the kingdom of God, but he will take seriously the prophetic warnings against all forms of domination and exploitation of the weak by the strong. He will try to discern the deeper meaning of the history in which he himself is involved. He will back every effort toward justice in all human relationships. Surely, God is as present in the history of our time as he was in the eighth century B.C. — for those who have eyes to see.

We stand in a period of drastic change, of tremendous possibilities and dangers. The dangers are written on the wall for those who dare to look at them. Americans will think immediately of the communist threat, but the greatest problem of the future might well lie in the growing bitterness of the colored races against the white race, of the "have-nots" against the "haves." People today do not want charity but justice. They claim the right for every man in a given country, and for every nation in the wide world, to achieve a normal standard of life. This concept still means for many the right not to go on half-starved while others are more than fed, the right to enjoy the benefits of education, the right to live as free and responsible men.

Does not our Western world stand under God's judgment in all this? Are not money and power the real gods to the service of which much of our lives is devoted? Is not the evil that is in the world today at least partly the result of past unrighteousness? Are not the birth and expansion of communism a consequence of the way in which Western Christendom in the nineteenth century has, with a few exceptions, allowed without protest the exploitation of the working class in the time of the industrial revolution?

Karl Marx was a Jew, with a messianic sense of justice, but unfortunately without the prophetic faith in God. He thought that a change in structures would be enough to bring about the happiness of man. Therein lay his error. Some Christians tried to raise their voice but were not heard. No wonder that the downtrodden heard the call of Marx and decided to take their own destiny in hand, for good or for bad. And we have been faced with the bitterness of class struggle. Justice is never trodden down without both parties involved having some day to bear the consequences.

Americans may say that their workers have today a fair share of the nation's goods and their own means of defense, and it is true that theirs is the highest standard of living. Still, however, the Americans have burning problems to solve, as do the Europeans also. Yet for both America and Europe the greatest problem today lies in the international sphere. It is our rich West as a whole; it is the white race as a whole which stands under God's judgment.

The judgment of men is never fair. The colonial period has had its positive sides as well as its cruelties; it was probably an unavoidable phase in the world's development. Military occupation and economic pressures, in spite of much suffering, can be forgiven. What is not easily forgotten, however, is what we have done to the human dignity of the Asian or the Negro or the Arab. These are the scars most difficult to heal. For Christians this is a problem of the first magnitude.

With understanding and humility we should face the bitterness of our brothers from other nations and races. We have all too long imposed on them our ways of thinking, our conception of life, without asking ourselves whether this was really what they wanted. The West holds such economic power that political independence remains meaningless as long as economic imperialism goes on and international trusts control the world markets.

What can we individual Christians do in such a situation? Is it not the business of economists and statesmen to find ways and means for improving the situation? Most problems today need to be dealt with on a world scale and call for the experience of the specialist. But too many financial and other interests are at stake, and the situation calls for such sacrificial measures by those in power that only a strong public opinion can bring them about. And who could help such an opinion to be formed and become conscious and vocal, if not the churches — especially in countries where the church is strong? The rank-and-file members have a deep responsibility as shapers of public opinion.

The World Council of Churches has a tremendous task to fulfill in this realm. What individual Christians cannot do, the concerted work of church leaders and expert laymen might achieve: They can stir public opinion, speak a word of warning, and point toward possible solutions. The

Assembly for Church and Society held in 1966 in Geneva was an important step in that direction. Of course there was no unanimity as to the possible remedies, but there was a common and earnest search for truth, a will to face the world situation realistically, a sense of responsibility shared by all participants. The presence of Christian delegates from Asia, Africa, and South America faced the Westerners with some provocative questions. And the quest for justice in both the social and the international realms was seen as one of the Christian imperatives for our day. But only as the rank-and-file Christians at the grass roots will share this concern will these issues be taken seriously by the statesmen of the world. In this buildup of opinion lies your task and mine.

Concerned Christians will never forget that sheer equity is a necessary beginning but not the ultimate end of the Christian endeavor; righteousness can only be fulfilled by vicarious suffering and love. Our world is hungry for justice but, perhaps without knowing it, still more hungry for love.

THE
QUEST
FOR
FREEDOM

FREEDOM IS ONE OF the favorite slogans of our time. People want to be free, though in actual fact there are relatively few people in our world who are really free. What people mean by freedom is not always quite clear.

Young people want to build their own life in their own way, and this is a perfectly normal desire. Sometimes, of course, they go too far. They want to free themselves from worn-out traditions, from a past that conditions their present. They do not always like the world that their elders have prepared for them, and unfortunately they may be right. They are aware that they live in a time of change; they question what they would easily call the prejudices of their elders: the creed, the morals, the way of life which the preceding generation has left for them. Young people want to be free for whatever the future may bring. Behind this call for freedom there is a restlessness which is typical of today. There has always been a conflict of generations, but the restlessness seems greater in our time — even to the point of purposeless destruction of property in which young people seem to feel the need to explode.

Young nations claim their freedom, meaning political

independence, of course, but also more than that. They also seek the freedom to build up their corporate life in their own way. Countries like France and the United States have fought hard for their freedom and they have instinctive sympathy for those who engage in a similar struggle. Every ship entering New York harbor looks at the Statue of Liberty as a symbol of the country it enters. The three words *"Liberté, Egalité, Fraternité"* ("Liberty, Equality, Brotherhood") are engraved on every French public monument. Logically, but not always accurately, we speak of our Western world as the "free" world, in contrast to all the right- and left-wing dictatorships.

Political freedom is a great gift; more, it is a necessary condition if a human society is to reach mature, responsible manhood. The Bible reflects this: Has not God delivered his people from the yoke of Egypt so that they may freely serve him? Their purpose was greater than political independence; it was freedom to serve God, but those hard-necked people often made use of their freedom by turning away from serving him.

The Bible shows that more than political freedom is required to make a free nation, and still more to make *free men.* Outward freedom is of little avail to those who are not inwardly free. The question always remains: *From what, for what,* are we free? Without this qualification, freedom is an empty word. In fact, it is a delusion.

In biblical terms freedom can be found only in fulfilling the destiny for which we are made. And because the Bible claims that we are made to love and serve God and that in him only shall we achieve fullness of life, it shows to us in our Lord Jesus Christ the very embodiment of freedom. He is totally free for God and totally free for his fellowmen, because the powers which hold humanity captive have no power on him. In the Gospel of John, Jesus reveals the secret of that freedom when he says, "The prince of this world . . . hath nothing in me" (John 14:30, King James Version).[1]

What do we mean when we speak of Jesus as a free man? It is not easy to put this idea in so many words. To open the Gospels is like suddenly breathing fresh mountain air after the stifling atmosphere of our cities. Jesus appears so marvelously free from all the prejudices and handicaps which we have to face in our daily relationships with our fellowmen. Look at Jesus sitting at the well and talking with the Samaritan woman. Both because she was a Samaritan and because she was a woman, no Jewish man will talk with her. But Jesus breaks the taboos by the simple act of asking her for a drink of water. Look at him also sitting with equal ease at the table of the Pharisee and of the publican. He is free for others, whoever they may be, and the others sense this unique openness to their needs and concern.

I can appreciate his freedom more fully by recalling how I felt when I was a young student secretary in Paris. I went down to a street where there were little cafes with curtains made of pearls hanging down. I used to think, "Jesus would go into places like these quite naturally and talk with the people there, but I cannot." I was inhibited, but Jesus was free. He could have sat with the people and talked with them to awaken in them a life which they did not know.

He is free from fear. He offers his life freely. He knows whither he comes and where he goes. And the secret of his freedom and fearlessness among men is his at-oneness with the Father. It is God's very freedom that shines through him. The call of Jesus is a call to freedom, that freedom he himself enjoys.

[1] The Revised Standard Version and certain other translations read "has no power over me," but I think that "hath nothing in me" expresses more strongly the fact that there is no Achilles' heel by which the power of evil can grip or master Jesus.

"If you continue in my word, you are truly my disciples, and you will know the truth, and the truth will make you free." . . . "Truly, truly, I say to you, every one who commits sin is a slave to sin. The slave does not continue in the house for ever; the son continues for ever. So if the son makes you free, you will be free indeed" (John 8:31, 34-35).

Jesus thus looks at man as captive: captive of his lusts and his fears, captive of his self-centered ego, and therefore estranged from God's life and God's love. And it is this estrangement, this lostness, that the Bible calls sin.

Jesus claims that those who stake their life on his word will *know*. This is no abstract wisdom, but *truth lived*; those who follow him will discover the deeper meaning of life. They will be faced with the reality of the God of love embodied in Jesus. They will look at themselves as they are. And this confrontation with the reality of God's mercy and their lostness will open the way to forgiveness, to the new life that Christ shares with those who follow him.

The Son is free because his obedience to the Father is the answer of love to love. The freedom of our Lord does not mean that he is less obedient, but rather that his obedience is spontaneous, the obedience of love. The Jews who oppose him are slaves of the law. Their self-righteousness closes them to that new life which the Son provides. Freedom appears here as the fruit of love. When we love someone we do things freely for him; but when we do not love somebody and out of a sense of duty have to do something for him, this compulsion prevents us from doing it joyfully, after the manner of saints. The secret of Jesus is the secret of selfless, self-spending love. This is the way of life he wants to share with those who follow him.

To know what the freedom of the children of God means, we need only to look at the apostles. Here are men who, during the earthly ministry of our Lord, were still confused and inhibited by doubts and fears — fear of the storm, fear of death, fear of the ironical judgment of their fellowmen. Think of Peter, who denied his Lord because of the questioning of a servant. And now these same men, standing in the strength of their risen Lord, filled with the power of the Holy Spirit, are ready to face trial and persecution. They stand before the Sanhedrin as men that no earthly power can silence: "We must obey God rather than men" (Acts 5:29). These are free men.

The apostle Paul goes from city to city, threatened, thrown in jail, beaten, and stoned. No power can stop him from proclaiming his gospel. The love of Christ burns in his soul, because this love has made him free. Free from what? To this he gives a twofold answer: free from guilt, free from the yoke of the law.

No man, perhaps, has experienced so bitterly the lostness of the best-intended human creature than did this staunch Pharisee who had tried so hard to comply with the old regulations of the Jewish law. Had not his zeal for the law led him to the worst of crimes, that of persecuting the Son of God? By the grace of God, however, Paul has experienced the miracle of forgiveness of sins; he is born to the free life of the children of God.

It is no wonder that Paul denounces legalism with the utmost violence. Legalism is a recurring temptation of the church in all times. It is so much easier to lay down a set of strict rules than to run the risk of faith in the guidance of the Holy Spirit. Let us therefore try to understand what Paul had in mind in his controversy with the Galatians.

This young church had received with joy the good news of God's love and the saving power of Christ. But people had come, probably some well intentioned and narrowminded Jews from Jerusalem, who told them faith in Christ was all right, but not quite enough. They had also to submit to the Jewish law. Unfortunately in the mission field today there is a similar problem caused by missionaries who come in and trouble people by telling them that what was taught by their predecessors was not quite the right thing.

Why does Paul react so violently in this angry letter? To him Christ is everything or nothing. We cannot be saved by Christ "plus something." To be baptized in Christ is to be born to the new life of the Spirit and to live that life in joyful freedom. To stick to the old crutches is to reject Christ's royal gift and seek again our security in human achievements. Paul pleads for the true gospel with an anxiety that the subsequent history of the church will fully justify, for there are many subtle ways of drifting away from the unique message of salvation by Christ alone.

> For freedom Christ has set us free; stand fast therefore, and do not submit again to the yoke of slavery. . . . You are severed from Christ, you who would be justified by the law; you have fallen away from grace. . . . For you were called to freedom, brethren; only do not use your freedom as an opportunity for the flesh, but through love be servants of one another. For the whole law is fulfilled in one word, "You shall love your neighbor as yourself" (Galatians 5:1, 4, 13-14).

Paul goes on showing that to be born of the Spirit implies walking by the Spirit and necessarily bearing also the fruits of the Spirit, which are love, joy, peace, patience, kindness, goodness, faithfulness, gentleness, and self-control.

The Christian whose life is grafted in Christ bears the fruits of the Spirit as naturally as the vine bears grapes. The image has been used by our Lord himself when he speaks of "the true vine." The one necessary thing is to "dwell in him." When Christian life is understood as a set of principles, of things to be done and not to be done, it is like an artificial Christmas tree on which apples and oranges are attached. It is not an organic living reality. A catalog of duties has been substituted for the free life of grace and love. We unavoidably begin to seek our salvation in our virtues.

It is strange that Protestantism, which started as a proclamation of salvation by grace alone, should have so often fallen back to a position in which not Christ but "Christian principles" are considered as the necessary guide in life. It is our subtle way of falling back under the domination of the law, and thus of finding our self-justification in our good deeds. There are people who claim to be good Christians merely because they accept a certain code of behavior. Morally they feel a bit above the average people. They are satisfied with this status, for they are "good people" who do not steal or murder and do (more or less) tell the truth. But are they committed to Christ?

Paul saw far and deep into the human heart when he warned his churches against these forms of self-justification based on good deeds. The glorious freedom of the children of God is a life lived day by day under the sign of God's forgiveness and mercy. This freedom certainly does not exclude self-discipline. Paul compares his life to that of the runner in the arena who drops all unnecessary equipment in order to run faster towards the goal (1 Corinthians 9:24-27). The love of Christ presses him forward, for Christ is his *raison d'être*, his goal, his very life. But he relies on Christ, not on his own virtues.

The one thing which matters is whether our actions draw us nearer to him or away from him. Thus, for a young person, the principle of living should not be "Don't do this" or "Don't do that," but "Does this thing estrange you from Christ?" or "Can you keep in contact with him while you do this?"

As the secret of the freedom of our Lord lies in his oneness with the Father, so does our freedom lie in our oneness with him, in our being conformed to his image. The mysterious work of the Holy Spirit is this remolding of our being, of our thoughts and ambitions, into his likeness.

In writing to the young churches which have grown out of pagan surroundings, the apostle deals of course with a number of moral issues. Guidance is needed in many areas. But whatever the issue, Paul always refers his churches first to Christ himself. The limits set to our freedom are those of love, of care for the weaker brother "for whom Christ died" (Romans 14:15; 1 Corinthians 8:11).

The example taken by Paul is that of meat sacrificed to the idols. If a man feels that to eat such food is against his conscience, those who feel free to eat it should abstain from tempting him. The concern here is that our attitude should not be a stumbling block for our brother. Our abstinence will never be a principle, but a free concession motivated by love. This same abstinence might be an offense for the pagan brother who invites us to his table.

Has not our Lord himself been accused of being "a glutton and a drunkard" because he was freely sharing the food and drink of tax collectors and sinners (Matthew 11:19)? For the Pharisees and other strict Jews, such a practice was impure.

Did not Paul blame severely his brother Peter for having suddenly abstained from eating with pagans in order not to offend some Jews who had come from Jerusalem and who did not accept that practice (Galatians 2:11-14)? Here the brother to be considered was the pagan newcomer to the faith, and the Jewish taboos had to be rejected in the name of our freedom in Christ. On other occasions Paul indicated that he knew how to be a Jew with the Jews.

This whole problem of freedom is a burning one today. The young generation is often reacting violently, even to excess, against Christian "moralism." Is it not true that we have sometimes reduced Christianity to a set of moral principles and failed to educate young people for authentic freedom in Christ? Some churches have set down the rule that a good Christian does not smoke or drink. Others would go further and condemn lipstick, dancing, and movies. We may abstain from all such things by inner conviction, but as soon as they become the criteria of being a good Christian, the whole axis of the Christian faith is displaced. We then have good reason to sympathize with those who revolt. We have surrounded them with barbed wire.

The child needs to be protected from mischief by putting barriers around him. As he grows, however, inner control is substituted for outward safeguards. Paul compares the law to the *pedagogos* who was in charge of bringing children to school. We have to be educated to freedom, and this is sometimes a difficult task for parents and teachers. We may start too early or too late. Only he who knows how to obey is ready for the kind of freedom the Bible advocates. The grown-up Christian still stands under God's commandments. The difference is that he obeys not under compulsion but freely, his urge being that of trust and love. Jesus makes this relationship clear when he says to his disciples: "No longer do I call you servants, for the servant does not know what his master is doing; but I have called you friends, for all that I have heard from my Father I have made known to you" (John 15:15).

Christian adult life is a free sharing in God's purpose for his world, a joyful acknowledgment of all he is and does, a free and trustful submission to his will. It may be costly, as it was costly for our Lord himself (Mark 8:32-42).

What exactly is a "free Christian" free from and free for? We have already mentioned that the main deliverance is the deliverance from guilt and from the weight of the law, but this implies a new attitude toward life. The freedom of the Christian means that he can leave the past behind and make a fresh start. This is God's great gift. Such a man does not look back at past failures, nor does he yearn for days gone. He is free for what the new day brings: "Forgetting what is behind," he "presses forward" (Philippians 3:13-14). Our Lord tells us that those who put the hand to the plow should not look backward, and Paul is writing in the same spirit when he says that he presses forward.

We know all too well how great the temptation is to hover on the past, on past mistakes, on past things which will never come back, on what might have been and is not. But a person with a free mind is one who rejects all useless worrying, entrusts the past and the future to God, and lives the day the best he can.

Modern authors have often described the tragedy of men haunted by a past from which there is "no exit," to use the term which serves as the title of Sartre's play. Sartre has seen modern hell as a hotel room where three people have to live together, each having a heavy past of which he cannot rid himself and each hating the others. This is a terrific vision of hell on earth. And in a very remarkable novel by Camus, *The Fall,* a man who thought he was good is suddenly confronted by an experience which uncovers all his egocentrism so appallingly that he cannot even cross a bridge without being tempted to jump into the river. But the Christian knows it is the mystery of divine forgiveness which breaks that spell, frees him from the despotism of his own cumbersome self, and makes a new beginning possible.

This knowledge means that we are *free for others* — free to listen, free to serve, free to love. Such freedom is a rare gift: We are more inclined to talk than to listen, to claim other people's attention than to try really to know them, sharing their concerns, their hopes, their sorrows. To be free for others means to be willing to meet them where they are, as they are, to respect the integrity of their being.

I read recently the confession of a Catholic missionary who tried unsuccessfully for ten years to teach the catechism to the natives of a certain African country. He had an utter sense of failure. After ten years, however, it dawned upon him that he should find out what *they* thought and felt. He started studying their life and customs, questioning them about their understanding of life, and suddenly doors opened. The people responded and a genuinely trustful relationship was built. This is a great lesson, not only concerning missionary methods but interpersonal relationships as a whole. This is what Paul means when he writes:

> For though I am free from all men, I have made myself a slave to all, that I might win the more. To the Jews I became as a Jew, in order to win Jews; to those under the law, I became as one under the law — though not being myself under the law — that I might win those under the law. To those outside the law I became as one outside the law. . . . To the weak I became weak, that I might win the weak. I have become all things to all men, that I might by all means save some (1 Corinthians 9:19-20, 22).

A great inward freedom is needed if we are to meet the other where he stands, rather than be a kind of chameleon, just taking the color of the place where we happen to be. It also takes a great love. It implies a will to understand the other's point of view, even at the risk of having to change our own. This is the condition of a free dialogue between men who stand in different walks of life. Our lack of freedom in our intercourse with other men is often a sign of our own uncertainty.

Nothing is more needed in our secular society, where so many men are detached from any professed faith, than men and women who are free from any inhibition in the professing of their faith, and who at the same time are open to the other, ready to listen — whether this other man be an atheist or a communist or anything else. It is possible to discuss the Bible with communists. This has been done frankly and openly in certain times and places, though of course it is more difficult in communist countries.

To think and act as a free man, furthermore, means freedom from *fear:* the fear of the morrow, the fear of poverty, the fear of illness, the fear of old age, and the fear ultimately of death. Many secret fears are nagging at our hearts that we dare not confess. We cannot get rid of them on command. They will vanish as our faith in God grows. We must confess them simply and humbly to him.

Another freedom greatly needed in our time is freedom from prejudice. We have in that realm the marvelous example of our Lord. How he broke through all the social and racial taboos of his time!

Daily propaganda strives to mold our thinking, to persuade us that our party or our country is right and all others are wrong. We naively believe we are free, but radio, television, and newspapers influence daily our thinking with a well-trained skill. The whole pressure of our time is a pressure to conform. The police states, whether of the right or of the left, have their own rough ways of imposing what they believe to be their interest. Our Western ways are more subtle, but in the long run they might be equally dangerous because of this very quality. We are gently molded into conformity with what the people around us think and want us to think.

Some time ago there appeared an interesting book by Riesman called *The Lonely Crowd*. He claimed that there were three main stages in human civilizations. During the first, the tribal period, man was "tradition-directed"; the elders set the pace for the young. In the second, the frontier period in America, man was "inner-directed"; the initiative and success belong to the self-made man. But now, says Riesman, we enter the third period, the "other-directed"; it is the group to which we belong which sets the rules. To conform to the group is, in a saturated society, the necessary condition of survival.

There is a great element of truth in this analysis. If America has been able to absorb so many migrants, it is because of the pressure to adopt the American way of life, the ability of the newcomers to conform. In a sense this is a positive value, and yet conformity may destroy our behaving as free persons. It is at this point that the Christian will have to make use of his wisdom. He will discern where to conform and where not. He will certainly not stand aside for the pleasure of doing so, but he will keep a free and independent mind where vital human values are at stake. He will "obey God rather than men." This is one of the most serious struggles of our time for the Christian — to keep inner freedom while the pressures get ever stronger.

The prophets of old were that kind of men. When God called them to speak his Word, they would stand up and no power could silence them, except by putting them to death. Fearlessly denouncing their rulers, they would proclaim justice and judgment.

The church in all times has had courageous voices, prophetic voices pleading the cause of justice, freedom, and mercy. I am thinking in our time of a Martin Luther King and so many others who have fought gallantly for racial cooperation, or denounced the evils of war. These are the kind of free men who are salt and leaven in a country's life. France had such men during the Algerian war; men who were courageous enough to denounce cruelties on both sides and to defend the oppressed. Because of this they were considered at the time as traitors to their country. But it is thanks to them that trustful relations can exist today between Moslems and Christians, Arabs and Europeans.

You might ask whether all this has anything to do with Christian freedom as shown in the gospel. Is there any relation between this inner freedom and all the political or economic freedoms for which the powers of the world claim to fight? I believe there is. Surely, a man can be in jail and remain inwardly a free man. Was Paul ever more free than when he wrote to the Philippians? On the other hand, political freedom does not necessarily make free men. We learn that fact every day in our so-called democracies, even though political freedom remains one of the most precious values of human life.

There are few truly free men in the whole world. Yet the whole Bible shows that God does not want a world of puppets, but rather a world of responsible men. He has paid heavily for allowing us to accept or reject his will. He does not enforce his rule on us, nor his love.

As Christians, we therefore must want men to be free to build up their own lives as they deem best, even if we believe they are on a wrong track. We know that every human being is a child of God meant to be not a slave but a man. We claim for everyone fullness of life, a fullness which implies freedom of choice, the possibility for developing the inherent potentialities they have, both as individuals and as members of a given culture or race. Our temptation is all too often to impose our own concepts, our own way of life on others who are not ready for it or do not want it. We are like parents who enforce on their children what *they* deem best.

Although our Western world claims to be the "free world," we must honestly ask whether it is really free. What about the propaganda which molds our thinking and often blinds us as to the real facts and the real motives of what is going on in the national and international spheres? What is the value of political liberty where economic pressures prevent a number of people from having a normal education and decent standards of life? Freedom implies the possibility to attain fullness of life.

The Christian who believes that God wants fullness of life for all his children cannot accept a situation in which certain groups in the population or certain parts of the world are maintained in what one might well call a subhuman condition. We shall not have a free world as long as some impose their way of life on others by outward pressure and even by military action.

This is a difficult and burning issue. It is my deep conviction that ideologies can only be fought and overcome by spiritual means. Our only chance to overcome communism, for instance, is to build up a society which combines the communist concern for social justice with a concern for personal freedom: what some of my friends like to call a "responsible society," where every member feels responsible for all and all for every one.

THE
QUEST
FOR
TRUTH

"WHAT IS TRUTH?" Pilate's question to Jesus (John 18:38) may express the skepticism of many Romans of his time. It certainly expresses the skepticism of a great many people of our own time.

Is there anything like a universal truth? Does not every religion, every ideology have its own conception of truth? Is there anything today one could call "scientific truth"? Has not every science its own limited field, its own methods of research, its own working hypotheses which, on experience, may prove true or false? Are we not moving toward a very empirical and relative concept of truth? No scientist today would claim to attain ultimate reality, even if such a thing exists.

The Greek word used in the New Testament which we translate by our word "truth" means literally "not hide anything." It means reality as over against false appearances, telling the truth as over against telling a lie. It can mean also a norm, the true measure of a thing, right behavior.

The biblical concept of truth could, in many cases, best be translated as *reality:* what is real, solid, binding, authentic. It is applied to an event which really happened, to a statement which corresponds to fact. In the realm of relationships it means truthfulness, straightforwardness, faithfulness. God is true because what he says, he does. He is utterly reliable. He keeps his word. He remains faithful to the covenant he has contracted with his people. Let us note here how close the meaning of truthfulness comes to that of righteousness which we have studied before.

Similarly, the trustworthiness of the man of God is measured by the correspondence between word and deed. When Elijah calls back to life the son of the woman of Zarephath, she says: "Now I know that you are a man of God, and that the word of the Lord in your mouth is truth" (1 Kings 17:24). The prophet of God speaks the truth; this means that what he says *happens*. This is what made the prophet both respected and feared. Jeremiah describes the false prophet as a "dreamer": His prophecies are so many lies (Jeremiah 23:16-32). The false prophet says only what people like to hear, and not the truth which could upset them.

The main quality that God requires in a man is truth, that is, sincerity, courage to look at things and at himself as they are and as he is.

> Behold, thou desirest truth in the inward being;
>   therefore teach me wisdom in my secret heart (Psalm 51:6).

> O Lord, who shall sojourn in thy tent?
> who shall dwell on thy holy hill?

> He who walks blamelessly, and does what is right,
>   and speaks truth from his heart;
> who does not slander with his tongue,
>   and does no evil to his friend,
>   nor takes up a reproach against his neighbor . . . (Psalm 15:1-3).

To walk with God is to walk "in the truth," for:

> The sum of thy word is truth . . . (Psalm 119:160).

Teach me thy way, O Lord,
  that I may walk in thy truth;
  unite my heart to fear thy name (Psalm 86:11).

The ordinances of the Lord are true,
  and righteous altogether.
More to be desired are they than gold,
  even much fine gold;
sweeter also than honey
  and drippings of the honeycomb (Psalm 19:9-10).

The wisdom literature, as found in Proverbs, is full of sayings about "lying lips" which are "an abomination to the Lord."

Truthful lips endure for ever,
  but a lying tongue is but for a moment (Proverbs 12:19).

The evil man moves in a world of lies; he hides from reality. He "does not know God."

Jeremiah sees one of the main signs of the sickness of his nation in the fact that there is no truthfulness in human relationships:

They bend their tongue like a bow;
  falsehood and not truth has grown strong in the land;
for they proceed from evil to evil,
  and they do not know me, says the Lord. . . .
Every one deceives his neighbor,
  and no one speaks the truth;
they have taught their tongue to speak lies;
  they commit iniquity and are too weary to repent.
Heaping oppression upon oppression, and deceit upon deceit,
  they refuse to know me, says the Lord (Jeremiah 9:3, 5).

How clearly in these words the ongoing march of evil is described: Oppression leads to deceit; and deceit closes the heart to God, because God is the God of truth. To face him is to accept the fact that one's heart is to be uncovered, and one's sin is to be acknowledged and confessed (Psalm 32:1-5).

When we turn to the New Testament we find that, for Jesus also, the worst of all sins is the lack of truthfulness. Our Lord is merciful in regard to the sins of the flesh: There is hope for any sinner who acknowledges and confesses his sin. A new beginning is possible. But what new beginning can there be for those who refuse to face reality, who deny the need for change? It is the most pious people of his time, the Pharisees, that Jesus judges with the utmost severity. Why? Because they claim to know God, but their life denies their words. More: By their hypocrisy they become a stumbling block to others, presenting to people a caricature of the God of truth and love. The 23rd chapter of Matthew, with its repeated cry of "Woe to you . . ." is the hardest pronouncement our Lord has ever made. These men hide their covetousness and thirst for human prestige under a cover of religious zeal. Religious deceit is the worst of all deceits. Its effect on the soul threatens to be deadly.

The Fourth Gospel gives a central place to the discussions between Jesus and the Pharisees, and the recurring problem is that of truth. Jesus claims to have come into this world to witness to the truth, but his opponents deny his authority. Jesus is shown uncovering the real motives of their opposition. They hate the light because their deeds are evil (John 3:19). They claim to be Abraham's children, but they reject all that Abraham has stood for, his straight and truthful relationship with God.

> Why do you not understand what I say? It is because you cannot bear to hear my word. You are of your father the devil, and your will is to do your father's desires. He was a murderer from the beginning, and has nothing to do with the truth, because there is no truth in him. When he lies, he speaks according to his own nature, for he is a liar and the father of lies. But, because I tell the truth, you do not believe me . . . (John 8:43-45).

These are harsh words. Why is the rejection of truth paralleled with murder? Jesus well knows that to a person who consciously rejects the truth, the presence of the man who embodies that truth soon becomes unbearable. Hatred is the seed of murder. It is the religious leaders who feel judged by the words of Jesus, and not a pagan crowd, which will put Jesus to death.

These are facts that we should always remember. Where faith is not truly lived, the religious institution can become more demonic than any secular agency. We have tragic examples of this fact in the history of the church. Many prophets, in all times, have paid with their lives for their proclamation of what they knew to be the truth. Let us remember, for example, John Hus and some of the later Reformers who became unbearable because they questioned the existing institutions so thoroughly that those who represented the institutions had to get rid of them at any cost.

The Synoptic Gospels show the crowds wondering at Jesus as one who speaks "with authority" and not as the scribes. He "knows." More: He does what he says. In the Old Testament the mark of truth is the perfect concordance of word and deed. God speaks and the thing happens (Psalm 33:9). The authority of the prophet depended on the actual happening of things he had prophesied. In Jesus, as in God, *thought, word, and deed are one*. He does not only announce deliverance; he delivers. He does not only preach the Sermon on the Mount; he lives it. He pays back love for hatred, life for death. His yes is yes. He is the man of "no hiding," and this concept is the meaning of the very word "truth."

The Fourth Gospel puts in so many words what is already suggested in the other Gospels. Jesus is the revealer of God's truth. He is truth itself:

And the Word became flesh and dwelt among us, full of grace and truth; we have beheld his glory, glory as of the only Son from the Father. . . . For the law was given through Moses; grace and truth came through Jesus Christ. No one has ever seen God; the only the dead, that in everything he might be pre-eminent. For in him (John 1:14, 17-18).

The coming of Jesus is compared in this Gospel to the light that shines in darkness. The property of light is to reveal what is hidden, to show things as they are. We think of the mystery of the dawn, when suddenly things that have been obscure now appear in their true form and color as the world emerges from darkness. What a marvelous image of the spiritual life!

Jesus "knows" what is in man. He uncovers the hidden thoughts of the heart, as X-rays reveal the hidden tumor; and, like many a sick person, we fear this revelation. To those who face reality this uncovering means their deliverance. To those who refuse, it means damnation in the technical sense of alienation from God. The Gospel of John reminds us of a certain painting by Rembrandt in which our Lord stands at the center in an orb of light with a crowd around him. All the faces which are turned toward him reflect his light which shines also in their faces, but those which are turned away from him are in darkness. The whole Gospel of John is intended to disclose in living reality the meaning of turning to the light and of turning away from it.

Thus truth appears not as an abstract concept, not in the form of an imposed creed or set of beliefs, but as a life lived. Truth is embodied in a Man in whom, through whom, the righteousness, the freedom, the self-spending love of God shines as through the most transparent glass. In the words of Jesus himself: "I am the way, and the truth, and the life. . . . He who has seen me has seen the Father" (John 14:6, 9). Christ himself, lighting our paths and showing the way to fullness of life, is the Truth.

Through his life, through his victory over sin and death, Jesus reveals all that we limited creatures can know of God as the Lord of life who wills life, not death, for all his creatures. At the heart of the universe there is a power of redeeming love, relentlessly at work, leading man to his ultimate destiny.

The God of Jesus Christ is not an omnipotent tyrant who imposes his will and destroys those who resist him. This caricature of God has unfortunately been widespread in Christian circles and has contributed to the skepticism and atheism we encounter today. No, the God of Jesus Christ is the crucified God who bears the plight of mankind but cannot force the heart of man to respond to his love. Imposed love would be a contradiction in terms. Speaking of his being lifted up on the cross, Jesus announces that it is from the height of this cross that he will draw all men unto himself (John 12:32). It is through this self-offering, through the life-giving Spirit that the stubborn resistance of man to the God of love will be broken.

The truth revealed on the cross is the ultimate victory of divine love over the powers-that-be. Love has proved stronger than hatred, life stronger than death. In the strength of this victory a new mankind is born, and the good news of Christ's victory and his life-giving Spirit will shake to the depths the antique world.

Buried with Christ and risen with him to new life in baptism, feeding on him through Word and Sacrament, the young church proclaims joyfully her faith and her expectation. As Christ is at one with the Father, so is the church to be at one with him and in him. As Christ is the man-for-others, so is the church meant to be a fellowship of love, ever open to the needs of every man. Truth is a reality to be lived in daily life, a venture in relationships.

The divine love of the Godhead — Father, Son, and Holy Spirit — is to be reflected in the life of those who belong to God. Therein lies the divine mystery of the church: the presence of the Holy Spirit.

Unfortunately, however, the church also remains a bundle of human beings who are still sinful, selfish human beings. Soon there arises the danger of substituting sheer intellectual knowledge for the deeper concept of truth as a reality to be lived. Intellectual thinking certainly has its important place — we could not do without theology — but there is a terrible and recurrent temptation to put a belief into the place of a life. Believing is easier than living. The First Letter of John denounces a group of people called Gnostics who, under the influence of current non-Christian doctrines of their time, claim to have attained wisdom. They are clever, a select group of people who know about God, claiming a specific revelation. But John denounces them as lacking the two essentials of Christian life: humility and love. With fierce vigor, John reminds them that truth is a reality to be lived:

> This is the message we have heard from him and proclaim to you, that God is light and in him is no darkness at all. If we say we have fellowship with him while we walk in darkness, we lie and do not live according to the truth; but if we walk in the light, as he is in the light, we have fellowship with one another, and the blood of Jesus his Son cleanses us from all sin. If we say we have no sin, we deceive ourselves, and the truth is not in us. If we confess our sins, he is faithful and just, and will forgive our sins and cleanse us from all unrighteousness. If we say we have not sinned, we make him a liar, and his word is not in us (1 John 1:5-10).

> By this we know love, that he laid down his life for us; and we ought to lay down our lives for the brethren. But if any one has the world's goods and sees his brother in need, yet closes his heart against him, how does God's love abide in him? Little children, let us not love in word or speech but in deed and in truth (1 John 3:16-18).

This is a great message, this First Letter of John, which is directed against the great heresy of its times, the heresy of a belief that would not be translated in terms of humility and love. This cocksureness, this belief that one holds the perfect truth, is present in all times, and people who hold it are tragically unkind in their judgment of others. They are so sure that they have the truth that they lack love.

The Holy Spirit is called "the Spirit of truth." He will guide the church and lead her to fullness of life. He will not speak on his own authority; he is the faithful witness of the risen Lord: "He will glorify me, for he will take what is mine and declare it to you" (John 16:14). The Spirit is both the counselor who will open the church to the mysteries of divine truth, and a life-changing power which enables the church to render witness in word and deed. If the voice of the church is to be heard today, the Spirit must blow on her as a life-changing power. There are too many meaningless words in life — in what we read and in what we hear on the radio, for instance. Words have lost their power if they are not translated in terms of life. We have to show the world that the Holy Spirit whom we confess is a life-changing power in our own lives.

Let us summarize our findings:

What the Bible means by truth is a dynamic, creative reality: the reality of a God who is Love communicating his life to men, calling them to share in this mystery of self-spending love and to grow in togetherness to that mature manhood revealed in Christ.

How does this concept of truth relate to the various concepts of truth we have mentioned in the beginning? to other faiths or ideologies? to scientific truth?

If we Christians recognize that God's divine love is at work in his creation, if we see in Christ the revelation and norm of true manhood, we shall rejoice at every sign of straightforwardness and mercy, at every earnest striving for justice found in men of other faiths or of no faith at all. The Spirit blows where it wills, says our Lord, and it may happen that an atheist may teach a Christian what it means to have true respect for others or, may outpass him in his struggle for social justice.

We should be ready, in all humility, to recognize in other men every genuine search for truth. We are not told who the people are that the Son of Man blesses in the Matthew story of the Last Judgment (Matthew 25:31-46). They come from many nations, and in the Bible this term implies the pagan world. All we are told is that they have fed the hungry, clothed the naked. Is it not possible that there are Muslims and communists who have met this requirement and therefore will be among the blessed? Christ regards these deeds of love as done to himself, because he has taken the place of each and every man on the cross. It is a consoling thought that some who have not known him may have nevertheless served him even without this knowledge but by some mysterious gift of the Holy Spirit. Christ is present in his world, working secretly in the hearts of people who do not yet recognize him.

On the other hand, this story of the Last Judgment also gives us cause for worry, for it reminds us of the missed occasions, the lacks of love, of which we are guilty. Christ will say to us, "This is what you have not done to me, whom you claim to love and to confess." Christ is present and regards as done to him everything that is done to harm others, whether to a Jew in World War II or to an African in Johannesburg or someone in Algeria or Vietnam. How many things all nations will have to answer for in the Last Judgment!

The only question we can ask ourselves, and it is a burning one, is: Do I live the truth I know in such a way that the nonbeliever will be attracted to the God of love I profess to believe in? It is on the sincerity and depth of our relationships that we will be judged.

Whenever we speak of truth, sooner or later we must take into account the scientific concept of truth. A Christian should never be afraid of honest scientific research. If we believe in God as the Creator of the world, every discovery can only increase our wonder, for how complex and mysterious is this universe!

The time is happily gone when the church could condemn Galileo for declaring that the earth revolved around the sun and not the sun around the earth. The Second Vatican Council has recognized in the name of the Roman Catholic Church the right of science to make free investigation in its own realm, and thoughtful Protestants have long accorded this recognition in less formal manner.

The conflict came from a mechanical conception of divine inspiration, by which it was claimed that the Bible could not err, even in matters of history or natural sciences. There are still some Christians who hold such views, and their position raises insoluble problems. But is not this a deep misunderstanding as to what the Bible means by divine revelation? The encounter of God with man is always an encounter with a concrete man of flesh and blood who lives in a given time and place. Miraculously God meets him where he is, in the context of a given culture. This man transmits his experience in his own language and in the categories of thought of his time. This is a condition for his being understood.

Archeological and historical research have helped us to see more clearly the kind of situation to which the writers of the biblical records addressed themselves, and thereby to understand better the message they were meant to convey. We know today that most of the books of this extraordinary literary collection we call the Bible are the result of a long maturation, the corporate witness of a people for whom life-with-God was tremendously real. The ancient traditions were reinterpreted and commented upon by successive generations, because it is always *today* that God calls his people to repentance and life. They did what every preacher does when he comments on the Scriptures: Past events become God's Word here and now.

Where historical research and exegetical work are un-prejudiced and do not reach hasty and unwarranted con-clusions, we should welcome them, even if they challenge at certain points our traditional thinking. A Christian should never be afraid of any honest quest for truth. He is ready to face reality in all realms of thought and life. Our fears always betray a lack of inner certainty as to the foundations of our faith. We need not be afraid of any discovery of science so long as Jesus Christ is our living Lord and Savior. This basic truth is the one thing science cannot destroy.

It is not science in itself we should question, but the use that immature men may make of scientific knowledge. It is the scientists themselves who warned the public against the use of nuclear fission as a means of destruction. Some-where I have read these words by atomic scientist Harold C. Urey, a Nobel Prize winner: "I write to make you afraid. I am afraid myself. All the experts I know are afraid." We are entitled to be afraid when biologists claim that by a manipulation of genes they might some day produce a superman, a superior race capable of dominating the world. We are entitled to be afraid when we see that by certain treatments one can scientifically break a man's will and make him confess crimes he has not committed. We are entitled to be afraid when we learn that a brain operation can change a man's personality. Here knowledge can be-come dangerous, even demonic, and destroy what is most precious in man: his free personality, his soul. The poten-tial of destroying the human psyche is indeed terrifying.

A Christian who has found in Christ the secret of full-ness of life will judge all things in this light. He will oppose those things which work against man's dignity and the freedom of man's personality. He will fight hard against all the lies which the press offers us so often in distort-ing the truth to make it more sensational. He will have to be aware that in relations between nations one of the main problems is the secretiveness of governments, which conceal their activities and distrust each other. The absence of full truthfulness in international relations is a great tragedy of our time.

The Christian will try to come as near to the objective truth as he can. He will not be swayed, for instance, by one newspaper, but will read a variety of publications to expose himself to differing trends and seek the real truth which lies behind the sensational reporting. He will welcome every step toward fuller manhood, every discovery which makes human life more livable, and he will stand up against every attempt to deprive man of his freedom and dignity.

Our time has tremendously increased man's knowledge, and we are told that the increases of the past twenty years are nothing in comparison with the next twenty. The whole question is whether man's spiritual maturity has grown in proportion and is capable of controlling the tremendous and dangerous forces his ingenuity has let loose. It is this spiritual maturity which should be the goal of every Christian, because the secret of true being is given to us in our Lord Jesus Christ.

CHRIST,
OUR HOPE

THE APOSTLE PAUL SPEAKS of the three greatest gifts of the Holy Spirit as being faith, hope, and love. We have considered faith and love. Let us now turn to hope.

Some people are very optimistic about the future of the world: They think we are entering an era of progress in which man, going from discovery to discovery, will soon master the world and his own life. But many others look more soberly at our world, seeing as many impending dangers looming at the horizon as there are reasons for hope. No matter how great the scientific achievements of man, still he cannot escape death. There is a widespread skepticism among our contemporaries about the beyond. "Let us eat and drink, for tomorrow we shall die!" is the unspoken motto of many people today.

The Christian is neither an easy optimist who refuses to look at the dark sides of life nor a pessimist who looks at the world as doomed. He is a realist, who knows the human heart; his hope does not lie in the achievements of man, though he is quite ready to acknowledge them. His hope rests in his faith in God.

We have seen how the prophets, in a very dark period

97

of Israel's history, had been given the vision of a new creation, the marks of which would be justice and peace. In their poetic language they see the wolf dwell with the lamb and the sucking child play over the hole of the asp. This new creation will come not as an achievement of man but as an act of God. And the instrument of its coming will be Messiah, the Anointed One on whom the Spirit of the Lord will rest:

> . . . the spirit of wisdom and understanding,
> the spirit of counsel and might,
> the spirit of knowledge and the fear of the Lord (Isaiah 11:2).

When Jesus appears on the scene of history, he proclaims that the expectation of the prophet is going to be fulfilled. Light has dawned on those who sat in the shadow of death (Matthew 4:16, Isaiah 9:2). In other words, the kingdom has "come near to you" (Luke 10:9). Jesus announces the kingdom that is to come, but this kingdom is already present, secretly present in the person of the Son of Man, even while it is still to come. Every healing, every act of deliverance, the mastery of the Lord over wind and sea, is seen as a sign and token of the kingdom to come. A time will come when man will be restored to wholeness, and his dominion over the created world will become wholesome and real.

Jesus announces that the Son of Man will come in power and glory as king and judge at the end of time, in accordance with Daniel's prophecy (Daniel 7:13-14). But the earthly way of the Son of Man will be that of the Suffering Servant, the way of rejection and death. The disciples, according to the Gospels, have never grasped this message during their Master's lifetime. When the crucifixion occurs, they lose all hope. The disciples on the Emmaus road confess sadly: "We had hoped that he was the one to redeem Israel" (Luke 24:21).

The decisive event is the resurrection. The certainty

CHRIST, OUR HOPE   99

that their Lord is alive changes a distraught group of dis-
illusioned men into a joyful, confessing church. The importance of this change is essential for any understanding
of the Christian faith. It is important to bear in mind
that our faith stands or falls with the belief in the resurrection. It is a dangerous illusion to believe that we can
save "Christianity" and drop the resurrection. Paul puts
this truth in blunt terms: "If Christ has not been raised,
your faith is futile and you are still in your sins" (1 Corinthians 15:17).

Because Christ has overcome sin and death, because he
is the living Lord of our lives, mankind has a *future;* death
is not the last word of our human destiny. An immense
hope runs through the apostolic message, that no human
power is able to quench. There was much skepticism among
the people at that time concerning an after-life, and there
is today. But this hope is not a kind of pious wishing. The
faith by which the apostles live and act is a driving power;
the Holy Spirit seals this faith in their hearts and bears
the fruits thereof. They taste the reality of the new life in
Christ; they are borne by his love; they grow into his likeness.

To be sure, the old self is not dead at once. It has been
condemned and crucified on the cross, and in faith Paul
looks at it as dead and buried, but he well knows that the
ultimate deliverance is still to come and yearns for the day
of fulfillment. He sees the whole of creation waiting for its
deliverance:

> We know that the whole creation has been groaning in travail to-
> gether until now; and not only the creation, but we ourselves, who
> have the first fruits of the Spirit, groan inwardly as we wait for
> adoption as sons, the redemption of our bodies. For in this hope
> we were saved. Now hope that is seen is not hope. For who hopes
> for what he sees? But if we hope for what we do not see, we wait
> for it with patience (Romans 8:22-25).

Here we have the paradox of the Christian life. Even as

Paul is thanking God that he is delivered by the risen Christ and belongs to him, still he is plodding along in faith waiting for his ultimate deliverance. And so are we carried by that faith in the victory of our Lord, who not only overcame sin and death on the cross but will overcome them in us; yet at the same time like Paul we are poor creatures plodding along toward our ultimate deliverance. Christ is our hope because in him we have the revelation of the full manhood that God wills for his children and the possibility of achieving it, and we look forward to the ultimate consummation with joyful expectation. One day we will know as we have been known, love as we have been loved (1 Corinthians 13:12). This is the hope that carries the apostle Paul through all the ordeals of his ministry.

John writes in similar terms to his "little children" in the faith:

> See what love the Father has given us, that we should be called children of God; and so we are. The reason why the world does not know us is that it did not know him. Beloved, we are God's children now; it does not yet appear what we shall be, but we know that when he appears we shall be like him, for we shall see him as he is. And every one who thus hopes in him purifies himself as he is pure (1 John 3:1-3).

This is a deep and mysterious passage. In it the hope by which we live is seen as a transforming power which in itself brings us ever closer to the goal.

It is said that when a couple have lived together for a lifetime in love and togetherness they sometimes begin to look a bit like each other; they have common features. Likewise if we look at our Lord steadily, something of his light will show in us even in this life. We may not see what has happened to us, but others will.

The apostolic hope is not limited to individual bliss nor even centered on it. The purpose of God embraces the whole of creation, and to be a Christian is to share God's concern for his whole creation. Paul speaks of the creation as being in travail. History has purpose and goal. It moves in a slow and mysterious march toward fulfillment. Sometimes in history there are obscure moments when we do not see clearly where we are heading, but still if we believe in Christ as *the* one in whom the whole of creation finds its meaning, we must believe that history has purpose and goal.

The Scriptures show Christ as the center, the beginning and end of all history. For in him, and in him only, does history take an ultimate meaning:

> He is the image of the invisible God, the first-born of all creation; for in him all things were created, in heaven and on earth, visible and invisible, whether thrones or dominions or principalities or authorities—all things were created through him and for him. He is before all things, and in him all things hold together. He is the head of the body, the church; he is the beginning, the first-born from the dead, that in everything he might be pre-eminent. For in him all the fulness of God was pleased to dwell, and through him to reconcile to himself all things, whether on earth or in heaven, making peace by the blood of his cross (Colossians 1:15-20).

In a few sentences the whole history of mankind is here seen and explained. Because Christ, the Son of Man, embodies the human destiny and at a given moment comes to fulfill it, history finds in him its meaning. This is certainly one of the most daring statements of faith ever made. The redeeming love of God as manifested in Christ is the *raison d'être,* the driving motive of history. To this end did all the galaxies come into being and start their mysterious rotations; to this end did the human being slowly emerge to consciousness and start his long march, not yet completed, towards manhood.

Redemption takes cosmic proportions. The universe becomes the framework where men of dust are being transformed into sons of God, and thereby attain what the New

Testament calls "mature manhood" (Ephesians 4:13). Could one imagine a greater vision of the destiny of man? The whole apostolic church looks forward in faith to this ultimate fulfillment: "We wait for new heavens and a new earth in which righteousness dwells" (2 Peter 3:13).

The church stands between the times, that is between Christ's coming in the incarnation, his victory on the cross, and his second coming in power and glory. The end is seen as both a time of judgment by fire and the ultimate victory of Christ over all the powers that be. Fire is the symbol of the purifying action of Holy God. The book of Revelation shows us the ultimate vision of judgment, the ultimate purifying, the ultimate deliverance — the vision of the city of God. Here is a vision of Holy God with no need for sun or moon because there is no more night. The glory of God shines over all creation and the slain Lamb is on the throne. All through this book we have had the terrible description of the powers that be, holding humanity captive, the power of the beast. The beast is overcome, not by military power but by the slain Lamb of God. Let us remember this vital insight, because this is how the beast is overcome in all times.

Why does eschatology, the doctrine of the last things, hold such a place in the Bible? Our tendency today would be rather to ignore this aspect of the Gospel. The images used are unfamiliar and unpopular. We have difficulty in imagining Christ coming on the clouds of heaven and the drastic description of the end in the book of Revelation is somewhat repulsive. Yet, through an imagery drawn from the apocalyptic traditions of first-century Jewry, we can grasp the deeper meaning of this expectation: namely that history moves towards a God-given end. In the vision of the City of God (Revelation 21), it is the slain Lamb who conquers the powers-that-be.

Our whole life takes its meaning from the end towards

which it strives. History makes sense only if we believe it goes somewhere and has an ultimate meaning, and we can only decipher the events of today's world in the light of such a meaning.

Our Lord tells us that those who seek first his kingdom will be free from the many cares of this world (Matthew 6:33; Luke 12:31). If Christ is our hope, our end, this goal will modify our whole attitude on daily life; it will determine what has priority in our decisions. It will liberate us, as we have already seen, from many unnecessary worries and make us free for what is worth our strivings. We live in a time of history when mankind is faced with a number of difficult choices. Old traditions break down; our community life undergoes drastic changes. Think of the movement of people from the rural areas to the cities . . . the problems of living in urban areas today . . . the breaking of the old community life of the village and the parish church . . . the loss of standing traditions in a mobile population. Where do we stand in this? Where *should* we stand?

The dangerous temptation is to look backward, to regret or try to maintain the past, especially in the church. Yet a Christian whose end is Christ does not look backward but forward. He knows that this world is in the making; he is open to all the possibilities of the morrow. He takes Paul's words as a motto: "Forgetting what is behind and straining forward to what lies ahead, I press on toward the goal . . ." (Philippians 3:13-14). Not the individual Christian only, but the church, is called to press forward to find new ways and means of meeting the needs, the searching questions of the average man of today.

A Christian will look realistically at the world as it is. Because he knows of human sin, he will not be overly optimistic as to human "progress." At the same time he will welcome and, if possible, back every effort made toward the improvement of human conditions of life.

The prophets saw in every crisis of history a foretaste of the end, a warning of impending judgment or a sign of the deliverance to come. If we look at our own time in this light, we see threats of moral decay within our advancing Western civilization: the crisis of family life with the breaking-up of so many homes, the growing racial and social tensions, the development of a technical society in which the personality of man is threatened by the anonymous character of the mass man who appears more and more as a cog in the machine. We hear the threat that brainwashing will change man into a puppet in the hands of a skilled police state, and the biologist claims that by clever handling he might be able to change man's nature.

The greater man's knowledge, the greater the threat, if he misuses his power. The Bible warns us that in the last times the power of evil will grow and the struggle between the forces of good and of evil will get fiercer. We can understand the wisdom of this warning as we see the life of the church deepening in our own day while simultaneously the adverse forces also gain in strength as the struggle gets harder.

At the same time the open-minded Christian will rejoice at every sign of human progress. Because Christ is his hope, he will welcome every step toward justice, every measure taken to improve the conditions of life of the less privileged, every act of mercy — whatever its source.

He will also remember, however, that every bit of human progress is limited and provisional. He will not stake undue hope on material improvements, nor expect a golden age to transform suddenly the condition of mankind. Such has been the naive hope of the communists and some humanists. In other terms the Christian will remember that the kingdom of God is not of this world. He will remember that man does not live by bread alone and that high standards of living do not necessarily bring happiness. At every turning of history, man has to choose between life and death, peace and war, mercy and ruthless destruction (or slow economic strangling of the helpless).

Those whose end is Christ know that ruthlessness and bloodshed will be answered for at God's judgment seat; and that the church which does comply with evil or does not denounce it betrays her Lord. Are we not, as the church of God, meant to be the light of the world and the salt of the earth? So Jesus has said immediately after the Beatitudes. We are to be this in two ways: by what we are as the church and by what we proclaim.

Are we not the company of those who live the new life of the Spirit, and have, through that Spirit, the tokens of the kingdom? Are we not, as the Body of Christ, to carry on his fight against all forces of evil and death? Are we not to follow the footsteps of the Suffering Servant, to reveal to the world the secret of selfless service, of vicarious love?

This we should be. But are we? Are we this fellowship of love that the world would envy and be attracted to, as the city on the hill attracts the lonely wanderer? Are we this holy priesthood which stands before Holy God for the whole world of nations in supplication and intercession and which stands before the world as the steadfast messenger of God's holy will and relentless love? Are we this "new race" (as Peter has called us), born from above, which brings into one fellowship of love men of all conditions, of all walks of life, of all colors of skin? How can we look forward to the kingdom of God? How can we be a sign of that kingdom and remain divided — split in ecclesiastical, or social, or racial factions?

All these questions burn one's mind and conscience. The first call of the church is surely to *be* the church, this visible sign of God's endless mercy in our torn world. We must reveal to the world the new kind of relationship that our Lord establishes between those who belong to him; between husband and wife, between parent and child, between manager and worker, between one neighbor or worker and another, and between different groups of nations.

If this new kind of relationship is not shown in our daily life, why should the world believe that the church has any message for it? There is a desperate longing for true community in our world. Riesman is right when he speaks of the "lonely crowd." Who is more lonely than the man in a crowd? Is not solitude the curse of our great cities?

The churches of the United States offer more warmth and fellowship than most of the churches in Europe. They have an amazingly friendly welcome. But the plight of modern man is such that we have to go beyond friendliness and niceness; we have to meet him in the depth of his solitude, of his search for the meaning of life. We must perhaps leave the comfort of the closed parish, to meet man where he works and strives. Here is the significance of the new type of group which is developing in our day — the professional group, the interest group, the group in which people find real fellowship and mutual help in their search for the meaning of life and the translation of convictions into daily living. These two realities, the life in Christ and the life of the world, need to be kept in communication with one another.

In Ezekiel 47 we have a magnificent vision of the river of life flowing from the altar of the temple into the world. As the stream goes on, it gets deeper and deeper. The stale waters of the Dead Sea are revived and the sea swarms with fishes. Wherever the stream flows, there is life, trees grow, bearing ever-fresh fruit. Is not this a beautiful symbol of the vocation of the church? We are no church if the life we receive through Word and Sacrament does not flow out into our surroundings as a vivifying power. Our Lord had certainly the prophetic image in mind when he proclaimed: "If any one thirst, let him come to me and drink. He who believes in me, as the scripture has said, 'Out of his heart shall flow rivers of living water'" (John 7:37-38). And John adds: "Now this he said about the Spirit, which those who believed in him were to receive . . ." (John 7:39). The Holy Spirit is the power through which the life of Christ flows in us and through us. It vivifies our relationships and gives meaning to our work and our leisure, as water vivifies the earth and makes it possible for things to grow and bloom.

The vision of Ezekiel has eschatological meaning. In the book of Revelation, John the Seer is shown the river of the water of life flowing from the throne of God and of the Lamb through the City of God. On either side of the river stands the tree of life, yielding its fruit every month; and the leaves of the tree are for the healing of the nations. All through the Bible we find this concern for the nations (meaning the whole pagan world).

Through the power of the Holy Spirit, the church is meant to bear the first fruits of the tree of life, but we are reminded that she can only do it insofar as her own life is continuously renewed at the source.

The local community thus appears as the sanctuary where we come together to worship and thank God and to receive from him the water and bread of life we are to share with our brethren in the outside world. An ingrown community which would seek fellowship for its own sake would soon be sterile. On the other hand, those who claim that they must leave the church in order to serve the world may soon present that world with stones instead of bread. It is from Christ, from his spent body, the church, that life flows.

What does it mean for a Christian of today to go "out"

into the world? It means that he will share the concerns of his fellowmen where human need or the dignity and freedom of men are at stake, whether this occurs in the professional realm or in the city. He will contribute to the building-up of secular groups where constructive action is needed. He is his brother's keeper, answerable to God for every wrong he has not tried to redress, for every suffering he could have attempted to relieve and has not.

The life of the church as a whole depends on the life of the local community, on the quality of love and brotherly service which radiates from there into the surrounding world. Important things happen at the grass roots. The tremendous problems which face our modern world cannot be solved by individual goodwill, however, nor by the local group. The world has become an intricate whole. No church, no nation can live in self-contented isolation. What happens in one corner of the earth may have repercussions of incalculable seriousness at the other end of the planet. The modern means of transportation and communication, with the spread of new techniques, have bundled us together, for better or for worse. The war in Vietnam is not an American problem; it has swiftly become a world problem which can set the whole of Asia and maybe the world on fire. So also with *apartheid* in South Africa.

It is generally agreed today that the greatest economic problem of our time, namely the growing gap between the rich and the poor countries of the world, cannot be solved by the goodwill or half-measures of some well-intended nations. The situation calls for drastic changes on a world scale, for an economic revolution in world markets, for a fairer distribution of means of production and basic goods of consumption. But all this change presupposes an awakening of the conscience of responsible citizens the world over — before it is too late.

Who will awaken the conscience of the world, if not the

church? Should we not see a gift of God's providence in the fact that in this century of unprecedented change and crisis the churches have been drawn the world over to overcome their divisions, to listen to one another, and to seek ways and means of common action?

Surely, there is still a long way to go. But what has happened in a short span of twenty years is far beyond what we could have hoped. We must see in the emergence of the World Council of Churches, and in the convening and decisions of the Second Vatican Council, action of the Holy Spirit. God in our time awakens his whole church to a new awareness of her mission in and to the world, and she discovers that if her call is to be heard, it must be issued in togetherness. The Spirit of God is strongly at work, but wherever such is the case, the devil is also strongly at work trying to stop him.

The churches have started moving. We can look back at John R. Mott, at the Faith and Order Movement, the Life and Work Movement, and now the World Council of Churches. Experts from all over the world have gathered under the auspices of the World Council, and tried to face realistically and constructively the great social, economic, and political issues of our day. We should not expect their findings to bring about sudden and sensational changes, but such efforts, if they are taken to heart by the rank-and-file Christians all over the world, hold the hope that new possibilities may emerge to move us toward a juster world. Courageous pioneers can do little if world opinion is not stirred and does not back them. Here comes our own responsibility as citizens of a given country, as members of a given church: to watch what is happening and try to integrate it into our thinking in the local church, in the limited sphere in which we have some possibility of action.

All this we shall do because Christ is our hope, because this is his world, because we believe that he is still relentlessly at work leading his creation to its ultimate goal, working through his church and also outside it through men who are concerned with justice and fairness.

And because Christ is our hope, our first and last word should be thankfulness:

Let us be thankful that he has placed us in this time of turmoil and change and called us to be co-workers with him.

Let us be thankful for the new techniques which tend to make life less of a burden for so many men and women and bring relief and new means of living to the less developed parts of the earth.

Let us be thankful that the present means of communication force us to think of mankind as a whole, so that where one member suffers, all suffer.

Let us be thankful that so many new nations have achieved at least a minimum of freedom and that others are on the way to it.

Let us be thankful for the growing thirst for human justice that one finds today in so many parts of the world.

Let us be thankful that the young generation rejects the *status quo* of easy conformity and wants to move ahead, even if it means some blundering.

Let us be thankful for every genuine search for truth, for the scientist and the artist and every worker who does his job honestly.

Let us be thankful for the signs of renewal in the various Christian confessions, for all courageous witness and every humble sign of love.

Let us be thankful for the ecumenical movement, for all joint efforts in prayer, witness, and practical service.

Let us be thankful because Christ, our hope, is stirring his church and his world to ever-new faith and action.

Let us be thankful, above all, because he, Christ, is the Lord of our life and of all life.